Also by John Gregory Dunne

DELANO

VEGAS

TRUE CONFESSIONS

QUINTANA AND FRIENDS

DUTCH SHEA, JR.

THE

STUDIO

John Gregory Dunne

New York
Limelight Editions

For Jean and Brian Moore

First Limelight Edition, March 1985
Copyright © 1968, 1969, 1985 by John Gregory Dunne

Manufactured in the United States of America

Library of Congress Cataloging in Publication Data
Dunne, John Gregory, 1932–
The studio.
1. Twentieth Century-Fox Film Corporation. I. Title.
PN1999.T8D8 1985   384'.8'0979494   84-26090
ISBN 0-87910-031-1

Foreword to the New Edition

I finished *The Studio* in the summer of 1968, but it was ten years before I actually read it. I did not read it in manuscript, I did not read it in galleys, I did not read it after it was bound. I disliked the book and at one point asked my publisher not to publish it.

I suppose the main reason that I disliked *The Studio* was that it was the only book I have ever written that went exactly according to plan. Before I started, I knew the voice I wanted: the omniscient cool narrator. I knew the style I wanted: short takes, shifting among a whole range of onstage and offstage characters. I knew where I wanted the book to start (at the annual stockholders' meeting) and I knew where I wanted it to end (at the premiere of a major motion picture). I needed only access; if I got the access, I knew I had the book.

The access was granted by Richard D. Zanuck, who was then the vice-president in charge of production at Twentieth Century Fox. There was no reason for him to give it to me, and to this day I do not know why he did; the nature of reporting is such that it certainly was not to his advantage to let me, or any reporter, see the inner workings of his studio. But Richard Zanuck did not hesitate for more than a moment after I proposed that he give me the run of the place. He called in his secretary and dictated a memo to all producers and department heads telling them to give me all the assistance I wanted. If they thought any information was privileged, they were to tell me it was off the record, or ask me to leave the room, location or set. It is an indication of the access I enjoyed that I was put "on hold" only once in the months I was at the studio.

I was given a parking space and an office, and a secretary to type my notes. I never availed myself of the last perquisite. It was several weeks before the personnel at the studio were comfortable in my presence, but after that I became as anonymous as a piece of furniture. My notebook was always out and visible, but I rarely took notes. After a meeting, I would race back to my office and transcribe the scene I had just witnessed—always in dramatic form; if a meeting or a confrontation was running long, I would duck into the men's room and jot down the things I wished to remember. Because I wanted no complaints that I had suckered anyone, I always identified myself and what I was doing.

Some months after I began my research, the studio's

vice president in charge of public relations came out to California from his headquarters in New York. He was appalled at the access I had been given and ordered it stopped. At a meeting in his office, he offered to buy me off, to make it "worth my while" to let the studio have editorial control over my book. If I refused, I would not be let back on the lot. I was in a quandary. I had no intention of giving up editorial control of the book, but at the same time I needed two set pieces—the preview of *Dr. Doolittle* in Minneapolis and the picture's premiere in Los Angeles—to complete the research on the book. I asked to see Richard Zanuck.

We had seen each other nearly every day I was at the studio, sometimes at lunch (I had a standing invitation at his table in the commissary), sometimes at dailies (I also had a standing invitation to watch the rushes with him). I told him that I could not in good conscience give him veto over the book and that, if that were the condition, I would pack it in. I suspect he wondered if I already had enough material to make a book; I also suspect he thought that throwing me off the lot at that late date would make any book I wrote less amiable. He finally asked if he could read the manuscript and make suggestions that I would be under no obligation to follow. I agreed. He ultimately asked me to delete three minor references. One—a producer's bad rapping of an actor—my lawyer had already said was libelous; the other two would have complicated Zanuck's divorce proceedings from his first wife. I made the deletions he requested.

The Studio was simplicity itself to write. It was mainly a matter of transcribing and rearranging my notes. That there were no surprises—I knew exactly what I was going to do—was for me the problem. Writing is essentially donkey work, manual labor of the mind. What makes it bearable are those moments (which sometimes can last for weeks, months) when the book takes over, takes on a life of its own, goes off in unexpected directions. There were no detours like that in *The Studio*. My notes were like plans for a bridge. Writing the book was like building that bridge.

When I finally read *The Studio*—I had picked it up because I had to check something in it—I was surprised at how much I enjoyed it. In the decade since I finished it, I myself had worked extensively in the movie business. Indeed, the first picture I wrote was for Richard Zanuck and Twentieth Century Fox. "Look," he told the producer, "do you mind if we don't mention *The Studio* in the announcement? It would make my life simpler." He remains the best executive I have met in the movie business, forceful and decisive. If he makes a wrong decision (and I think he might like to reconsider opening up Fox to me), he sticks by it, never apologizing, never explaining. That I had written *The Studio* was one thing; that I had now written a screenplay ready to go into production was another altogether.

If I were writing *The Studio* today, I would probably be more compassionate, but that is a factor of age and experience. The story of Henry Koster's meeting with Zanuck troubles me more than anything in the book, yet I think I would probably still put it in: a fact of the movie business is that people are used and discarded like so many wads of Kleenex. I would also change a nuance here and a nuance there, largely because I am convinced that it is impossible for anyone who had never worked in the movie business to understand the dynamics of any given picture. But on the whole, I am surprised and a little gratified at how accurate the portrait remains. In some circles, it is an article of faith that Hollywood is dead, the studios extinct. To which I can only say rubbish. Movies must still be financed and distributed, and they are still largely financed and wholly distributed by the major motion picture companies. If there are fewer pictures, the stakes are higher. A film like *Star Wars* can redeem the mistakes of ten years. Richard Zanuck was fired by his father at Fox; he went to Warner Brothers and was fired there. He formed an independent production company, went to Universal and co-produced *Jaws*, which probably has made more money than all the films his father produced personally in a lifetime.

Hollywood is a technological crapshoot. Table stakes open at a million dollars. It was true in 1968, it is true now.

I suppose that is why after seventeen years I like *The Studio* now. I got it right.

Los Angeles
January 1985

The characters

DARRYL F. ZANUCK, president, Twentieth Century Fox Film Corporation

RICHARD D. ZANUCK, his son, executive vice president in charge of world-wide production, Twentieth Century Fox Film Corporation

And in Alphabetical Order

MORT ABRAHAMS, associate producer of *Dr. Dolittle*

IRWIN ALLEN, a science-fiction entrepreneur

JULIE ANDREWS, a film star

EDWARD ANHALT, a screenwriter

ARMY ARCHERD, a gossip columnist

TED ASHLEY, president of the Ashley-Famous Artists Agency

GEORGE AXELROD, a Renaissance Man

JACK BAUR, assistant head of the Studio's casting department

PANDRO S. BERMAN, a film producer

JOEY BISHOP, a television personality

JACQUELINE BISSET, an actress

PAUL BLOCH, press agent

JOHN BOTTOMLY, technical advisor on *The Boston Strangler*

LESLIE BRICUSSE, scenarist-composer-lyricist, *Dr. Dolittle*

DAVID BROWN, husband of Helen Gurley Brown and the Studio's vice president in charge of story operations

ROBERT BUCKNER, producer

REGGIE CALLOW, assistant director of *Star!*

CAROL CHANNING, an actress

GEORGE CHASIN, partner in the Park-Chasin-Citron Agency

CHER, as in "Sonny & Cher"

CURT CONWAY, New Talent School

GARY CONWAY, a television actor

ALEXANDER COURAGE, co-arranger of the score of *Dr. Dolittle*

WARREN COWAN, partner in the public relations firm of Rogers, Cowan & Brenner

TONY CURTIS, a film star

PAMELA DANOVA, New Talent School

BOBBY DARIN, singer

JOHN DE CUIR, production designer of *Hello, Dolly!*

JAMES DENTON, the Studio's head of West Coast publicity

BOB DENVER, an actor

ABE DICKSTEIN, the Studio's head of domestic sales

LOU DYER, a Studio press agent

JAMES FISHER, the Studio's West Coast story editor

BERNARD FLATOW, head of Latin American publicity

RICHARD FLEISCHER, director of *Dr. Dolittle* and *The Boston Strangler*

HENRY FONDA, a film star

KURT FRINGS, an agent

WILLIAM FROUG, a television writer

ROBERT FRYER, producer of *The Boston Strangler*

PHIL GERSH, an agent

HAPPY GODAY, a song plugger

JOYCE HABER, a gossip columnist

SHEILA HACKETT, assistant to Michael Kidd

LINDA HARRISON, an actress in the New Talent School

REX HARRISON, a film star

HARVEY HART, director of *The Sweet Ride*

DALE HENNESY, a Studio art director

HAL HERMAN, television production manager

CHARLTON HESTON, a film star

JACK HIRSHBERG, a Studio press agent

STANLEY HOUGH, head of the Studio's production department

ARTHUR P. JACOBS, producer of *Dr. Dolittle*
GENE KELLY, director of *Hello, Dolly!*
MICHAEL KIDD, choreographer of *Star!* and *Hello, Dolly!*
HENRY KOSTER, director of *A Hundred Men and a Girl*
ERNEST LEHMAN, writer-producer of *Hello, Dolly!*
PERRY LIEBER, former head of West Coast publicity
FRANK MC CARTHY, a film producer and friend of General Omar Bradley
MARY ANN MC GOWAN, secretary to Richard Zanuck
HARRY MC INTYRE, a Studio executive
BARBARA MC LEAN, head of the Studio's cutting department
OWEN MC LEAN, head of the Studio's casting department
TED MANN, a Minnesota theater magnate
IRVING MANSFIELD, husband of Jacqueline Susann
DANIEL MASSEY, an actor
ARNOLD MAXIN, a music publisher
LOUIS MERMAN, assistant head of the Studio's production department
PAUL MONASH, a film and television producer
FRANK NEILL, a Studio press agent
LIONEL NEWMAN, head of the Studio's music department
JOE PASTERNAK, producer of *The Sweet Ride*
DAVID RAPHEL, vice president in charge of international sales
DON RECORD, a title designer
JERRY REYNOLDS, an engineer from the Boeing Aircraft Corporation
JONAS ROSENFIELD, the Studio's vice president in charge of publicity
ED ROTHMAN, an agent for Ashley-Famous Artists Agency
FRANKLIN SCHAFFNER, director of *Planet of the Apes*
IRENE SHARAFF, costume designer of *Hello, Dolly*

THE STUDIO

RICHARD SHEPHERD, an agent for Creative Management Associates

SPYROS SKOURAS, chairman of the board, Twentieth Century Fox Film Corporation

MILT SMITH, a Studio press agent

HARRY SOKOLOV, executive assistant to Richard Zanuck

SONNY, as in "Sonny & Cher"

BARBRA STREISAND, a film star

JACQUELINE SUSANN, an authoress

NATALIE TRUNDY, friend to Arthur Jacobs

DAVID WEISBART, producer of *Valley of the Dolls*

ELMO WILLIAMS, producer of *Tora, Tora, Tora*

ROBERT WISE, director of *Star!*

EVARTS ZIEGLER, partner in the Ziegler-Ross Agency

FRED ZINNEMANN, a film director

As a story it was reasonable enough to pass, and I sometimes believed what I said and tried to take the cure in the very real sun of Desert D'Or with its cactus, its mountain, and the bright green foliage of its love and its money.

Norman Mailer, *The Deer Park*

THE STUDIO

1

❝ *And now he's working for me,* **❞**

Darryl Zanuck said

Shortly after two o'clock on the afternoon of May 16, 1967, Darryl F. Zanuck stepped out of an elevator on the eighteenth floor of the Waldorf-Astoria Hotel in New York. He was wearing sunglasses and smoking a large black cigar and in the lapel buttonhole of his well-tailored blue blazer was the rosette of the *Legion d'Honneur*. In his wake, stopping when he stopped, walking when he walked, trailed a convoy of equally well-tailored men in the employ of the Twentieth Century Fox Film Corporation, over whose annual stockholders' meeting Zanuck was scheduled to preside that afternoon in the Waldorf's Starlight Roof. Leading the convoy, but a half step behind his father, the dauphin to the king, was Zanuck's only son, Richard Darryl Zanuck, a member of the board of directors of the Twentieth Century Fox Film Corporation and the Studio's Los Angeles-based executive vice president in charge of world-wide production.

As Darryl Zanuck entered the meeting room, a number of stockholders rose and began to applaud. The elder Zanuck paid no attention, and he seated the young woman with him, a slender French girl in a green silk Pucci dress, in a chair at the rear of the room. Then he headed for the dais, shaking hands with board members and embracing old friends as he went. Over the dais hung the green, gold and black flag of the Twentieth Century Fox Film Corporation. Already in his place at the end of the front table on the dais was Fox's chairman of the board, Spyros P. Skouras. During the years when Darryl Zanuck held the same post his son holds now, Skouras had chaired these annual meetings, but on this afternoon, he sat impassively, looking like an aging white-maned lion, his hands folded in front of him.

Darryl Zanuck took his place at the lectern, his son in a chair immediately to his right. The cigar was still implanted in Darryl Zanuck's mouth. "Well, here we go again," he said to Richard Zanuck. The microphone picked up his nasal Nebraska twang and there was a titter from the audience. Darryl Zanuck glared impatiently and then called the meeting to order, placing the agenda in front of him. Suddenly he stopped and took off his sunglasses.

"Are these the right goddamn glasses?" he said. "For Christ's sake, no."

He replaced the sunglasses with reading glasses and began to introduce the members of the board and Studio executives sitting on the double-tiered dais. When he came to his son, he stopped, fumbling for effect: "On my right, I can't remember his name, heh, heh, now I've got it, Richard Zanuck."

There was an appreciative laugh from the audience. Darryl Zanuck continued the introductions. "At the end of the table, a man—I worked for him once, I over-threw him once, I took the company away from him once, and now he's working for me, but I still have the greatest affection for him, Mr. Spyros Skouras."

Spyros Skouras did not move a muscle.

Each stockholder attending the meeting had been provided with a thirty-two-page four-color annual report which attested to Twentieth Century Fox's robust financial health. *The Sound of Music,* with a gross approaching $100 million, was the most successful film in motion picture history, there were over thirty other feature films in various stages of production, and the television department had ten shows totaling nine hours of prime-time viewing on the network airwaves. Gross revenues of the company were $227,259,000 for fiscal 1966, earnings before taxes $23,763,000, net earnings after taxes $12,504,000, earnings per share of stock $4.28. Richard Zanuck's salary was $150,000 with an additional $150,000 a year deferred; one television producer was being paid $435,000 a year, another $365,000 a year.

With the reading of the financial statement, the meeting was thrown open for questions. There were no complaints from the stockholders. A resolution was introduced praising Darryl Zanuck for his running of the company. Less than two hours after it began, the annual meeting of the Twentieth Century Fox Film Corporation was adjourned.

Five years before, the Twentieth Century Fox Film Corporation had been flat on its back. In 1962, Fox lost $39.8 million after taxes, and in the three preceding years the company had lost an additional $48.5 million in feature film production. To keep itself going, the Studio had sold 260 of its 334 acres just outside Beverly Hills to the Aluminum Company of America for $43 million. In Rome, production had started on *Cleopatra,* which began to sop up money faster than Fox could pour it in. The Studio was dying. Bankruptcy threatened, the sound stages were closed, the parking lots were empty. Spyros Skouras was fired as president, and Darryl Zanuck, after first threatening a proxy fight, was elected to take his place and save the sinking ship.

The reversal of fortunes of the Twentieth Century Fox Film Corporation had long interested me, for the vicissitudes of that studio seemed to suggest not only the *modus operandi* of all studios, of all motion picture people, but something else as well: I had the feeling that by spending some time at the Studio I could get close to the texture of life in the subtropical abstraction that used to be called The Motion Picture Capital of the World; that by watching motion picture people at work I could see and perhaps understand their ethic. I had been exposed to the motion picture industry at oblique angles ever since I arrived in Los Angeles in 1964, and some of its working arrangements seemed to me far more magical than that glamour for which the Industry was noted: there was the way in which failure escalated the possibilities of success, the way in which price bore no relation to demand. There was the way in which millions of dollars were gambled on ephemeral, unpredictable and, uncomfortably often, invalid ideas of marketability. There was the way that many, perhaps most, people in the Industry remained unconscious of their own myths and superstitions. There was the Eldorado mood of life in the capital, the way in which social and economic fortunes could shoot up or plummet down, as in a mining boom town, on no more than rumors, the hint of a rich vein, the gossip that the lode was played out.

All this seemed interesting to me, and not entirely for its own sake: the truly absorbing aspect of the motion picture ethic, of course, is that it affects not only motion picture people but almost everyone alive in the United States today. By adolescence, children have been programmed with a set of responses and life lessons learned almost totally from motion pictures, television and the recording industry. It is difficult to banish the notion of one's own life situations as part of a scenario, appropriately scored: "Lara's Theme" for an ill-starred love, "Colonel Bogey's March" for indomitable courage, "Waltzing Mathilda" for bittersweet apocalypse. Few situations fail to evoke a cinematic response; in matters of principle we play *High Noon*, in renunciation scenes *Casablanca*. ("Walter, Barton T. Keyes is a great man," Edward G. Robinson says about himself to Fred MacMurray in *Double Indemnity*, and whenever I am feeling particularly pleased with myself, the line

comes back.) In pictures, there is no problem without a
solution: the Mafia has been cut down to size at every
studio from Burbank to Culver City; Gregory Peck has
personally taken on anti-Semitism, the Bomb, and
Southern bigotry, licked them all, and we all feel, however spuriously, the better for it.

Movies, moreover, have given most Americans their
entire fix on how other Americans live. How many of us
grew up thinking of the medical profession in terms of
Not As a Stranger, of the literary life as *The Snows of
Kilimanjaro,* of heroin addiction as *The Man with the
Golden Arm?* The South was *Gone with the Wind,* and
later *The Long Hot Summer;* the Catholic priesthood,
Going My Way. For the socially mobile, movies have
constituted an infinitely accessible, if infinitely inaccu-
rate, primer in traditional social behavior. This very in-
accuracy of social milieu in Hollywood pictures—the
rich in Southampton do not wear white dinner jackets
in the summer (*From the Terrace*), United States Sen-
ators do not drive Rolls-Royces (*Seven Days in May*),
army officers do not salute as if they are hailing a cab,
nor do they allow enlisted men to call them by their first
names (any picture about the military)—seemed to
suggest that Hollywood lives at a considerable remove
from the rest of the society, lives and thrives entirely on
its own myths. In some ways Hollywood seemed a perfect example of a closed and inbred society, and the
Twentieth Century Fox Film Corporation, not long ago
on the brink of ruin, now the most successful studio in
Hollywood, itself shored up by all the basic tenets of the
Industry, seemed the best place to observe it in action.

And so, some time ago, I arranged to follow the Studio's activities over the course of a single year, to see how some of the people there got along, got ahead, fell behind, stayed in place, and, above all, fabricated the myth. What I hoped to find at the end of that year was something of the state of mind called Hollywood.

The day I arrived in the small austere lobby of Fox's administration building in Los Angeles, an elderly Studio policeman stood guard behind a glassed enclosure, examining each person entering the building before pressing a button opening the door into the Studio's inner sanctum. Beside him was a clipboard on which was written:

North Reception
Pico Time Gate

    Okays for Monday March 22
      26 musicians Stage 1, 1 P.M.
    Duke Goldstone Party to Peyton Place

    New Gate Okays
      Alex Cord—actor
      Gila Golan—actress

    Sonia Roberts TV writer will be in 22 Old Writers
    Peggy Shaw TV writer will be in 21 Old Writers

    The following will be pulled from files
      Thomas, Jerry—TV writer

Richard Zanuck's office is just across the hall from his father's, but at that time, the elder Zanuck had not once returned to Hollywood since he had taken over the Studio. He preferred to remain in New York where the books are kept and the financial decisions made, leav-

ing the picture making to his son. The suite occupied by
Richard Zanuck is cavernous. It is dark-paneled and on
the wall hang art department sketches of forthcoming
Fox productions. Behind his desk, in a gold frame,
there is a color photograph of his ex-wife, Lili, and
their two daughters, Virginia and Janet, as well as
two pairs of bronzed baby shoes. There is no hint of
show business in the office, no framed *Variety* headlines, no pictures of movie stars with fulsome messages
of endearment, no sentimental props from old Fox
films. On the mantel over the fireplace there is a four-
clock console, showing the time in Los Angeles, New
York, London and Paris, and in the adjoining bar-dress-
ing room are leatherbound scripts of all the pictures
Fox has made since Richard Zanuck took over as production chief. The anonymity of the office is in a way
reflective of what it means today to be a production
chief in the new Hollywood, dominated as it is by the
independent producers. As much as is possible, Richard
Zanuck tries to function by the rules prevailing in
Hollywood before the independents took over, guarding
Fox's slowly eroding right to shape every picture from
story conference to cutting room. But it is virtually impossible today for a production chief to put his personal
stamp on a picture in the way that Darryl Zanuck did.
He is, in many ways, a traffic manager, whose flexibil-
ity of action is far more limited than that of, say, the
chief executive of an automobile company. Instead of
assembling a "package"—story, talent, director, producer—he is more apt to be *presented* with one, take it
or leave it. If he takes, which means putting up the
money and providing the facilities, and he ends up with
a *Lord Jim*—Hollywood's equivalent of the Edsel—his

job is in jeopardy, although he had almost nothing to do with the making of the picture.

Richard Zanuck shook my hand and asked his secretary to bring us each a cup of coffee. He is a tightly controlled man with the build of a miniaturized halfback, twelve-month tan, receding brown hair and manicured fingernails that are chewed to the quick. He has hesitant blue eyes, a quick embarrassed smile and a prominent jaw whose muscles he reflexively keeps knotting and unknotting. He was wearing a monogrammed Sulka shirt and a gray hopsack suit. He blew on his coffee to cool it, and as he sipped, he reflected on the state of the Studio when he took over in 1962.

The demise of Fox had actually begun a half dozen years before, in 1956, when Darryl Zanuck had resigned as vice president in charge of production. The elder Zanuck was a tycoon in Hollywood when the title carried with it feudal power and virtual *droit de seigneur*. He came out of Nebraska after World War I, parlayed a novel which was underwritten by a patent medicine maker into a Hollywood writing job, wrote a series of films for Rin Tin Tin, became production chief at Warner Brothers at twenty-four, and founded Twentieth Century Fox with Joseph Schenk at thirty-one. "He has so many yes-men following him around the Studio," Fred Allen once observed, "he ought to put out his hand when he makes a sharp turn," but he won three Academy Awards and two Irving Thalberg Awards and came closer to the ideal of Thalberg (the prototype of Scott Fitzgerald's last tycoon, Monroe Stahr) than any other Hollywood mogul.

But the advent of television, in 1948, had changed the face of Darryl Zanuck's Hollywood. Weekly audi-

ences shrank from a peak of 90 million customers in
the halcyon days to 30 million, and feature film production fell from a high of 600 a year to less than 150.
With production so sharply curtailed, the studios were
no longer able to keep under contract a complete roster
of stars, producers, directors and writers. Independent producers moved into the void and agents became
the new czars of Hollywood, allocating to their clients
the profits and perquisites that once had belonged solely
to the studios. The changes dismayed Darryl Zanuck,
and he quit as Fox's production chief, went to Paris and
formed an independent production company. Richard
Zanuck joined him there as a story and production assistant.

The younger Zanuck was born in 1934. There was no
paternal coddling. Even when his son was a child,
Darryl Zanuck took delight in trouncing him at check-
ers. Nor was Richard Zanuck allowed to win a point at
badminton until he was big enough to ram the shuttle-
cock down his father's throat. He attended Harvard Military School in Los Angeles and after that graduated
from Stanford. Summers he worked at the Studio, first
on the labor gang and in the editing room, then in the
advertising department in New York, and finally in
Paris, as his father's assistant. In 1959, tied up in Africa with another picture, Darryl Zanuck gave his son a
chance to produce *Compulsion*, a fictional re-enactment
of the Leopold-Loeb case. Richard Zanuck brought
Compulsion in under budget, ahead of schedule and
good enough for its two stars, Bradford Dillman and
Dean Stockwell, to win best acting awards at the
Cannes Film Festival.

Meanwhile, back in the U.S., Twentieth Century Fox had fallen on lean days. Management was ineffectual and the production reins finally passed to Spyros Skouras, the Greek theater owner and company president who had always been content in the past to watch the books and let Darryl Zanuck supervise the picture making. At a time when other studios were retrenching in the face of television, Skouras pushed through dud after dud; with the sale of the back lot and the debacle of *Cleopatra,* the company was in a state of financial ruin. Then, after repeated absences, Marilyn Monroe was fired off a picture called *Something's Got to Give* and she went home and not too long afterward committed suicide. The picture was scrapped for a $2 million loss. It was the last straw. The board of directors issued a terse, three-paragraph announcement saying Skouras had been forced to "resign" because of "ill health."

From his headquarters in Paris, Darryl Zanuck, who was drawing a $150,000 annual consultant's fee from Fox, watched the company scramble for a new management. His family's large bloc of Fox stock—something in the vicinity of 100,000 shares—seemed in danger of going down the drain, as did his own production of the World War II epic, *The Longest Day,* which he had planned to release through Fox as a hard-ticket, roadshow picture, but which the panicked studio was preparing to saturation-book across the country. "I looked around for someone to recommend to them," he said later, "but found no one who would be an improvement." Except himself.

Zanuck's announcement of his candidacy stirred no

enthusiasm on the board of directors, which was concerned with his profligate ways in both his business and private lives, and lines were drawn for a proxy fight. The prospect of a destructive proxy battle, however, was far less tolerable to Fox stockholders than the return of Darryl Zanuck. Whatever his faults—and his rivals took pains to chronicle in detail Zanuck's romantic interludes and the millions he spent in abortive efforts to make stars out of such former consorts as Bella Darvi and Juliette Greco—Zanuck at least offered a lifetime of film knowhow, experience totally lacking in the bankers and brokers who opposed him. The stockholders threw their support to Zanuck and the board backed down, naming him president and relegating Skouras to the figurehead post of chairman of the board. There was still the matter of the new production chief. "D.Z. asked me who I thought was best qualified," Richard Zanuck recalls. "And I told him. Me."

Immediately after taking over as president, Darryl Zanuck shut the Studio down, fired most of its personnel, and threw out all the story properties bought by the previous management. The only production activity was one television show then in the dying days of its run. "It was desperate," Richard Zanuck said. There is a strained quality in his voice that becomes a slight rasp when he gets impatient. "There were only about fifty people here—everyone else had been canned—and we just sat around looking at each other. We closed down the commissary to save money, and everyone—secretaries, producers, carpenters—ate lunch in a little electricians' shed. It's an awful thing to say, but things were so tight, we were trying to figure out ways to get another janitor off the payroll."

Zanuck fingered one of the bronze baby shoes. There were charges when he took over the Studio that his appointment was due only to Hollywood's tribal law of primogeniture. The accusations of nepotism did not disturb him. "Quite frankly, naming me as production chief made a lot of sense," he said, draining the cup of coffee. "As the largest stockholders, my family stood to lose the most if the company went under. What nearly killed this company was the politics, the antagonism between the money people in the East and the picture people out here. With D.Z. in New York and me out here, that antagonism is gone now."

Like almost everyone brought up in the movie industry, Richard Zanuck is almost immune to the world outside. He reads voraciously, but mainly scripts, and his mind is an encyclopedia of plots, gimmicks and story angles. No detail escapes his attention. "How about a midget for the shoeshine boy?" he asks the director of a thriller. "There's something insidious about a midget." A producer's suggestion that an actor in a Western wear a mustache gets a quick veto. "We had a picture here once, *The Gunfighter*, with Greg Peck, and it bombed out. You know why? Peck wore a mustache." (Zanuck was thirteen when *The Gunfighter* was released.) He mentions a Gary Cooper comedy shot at the Studio years before. "Good picture," he says, "but small hat. You could never put Coop in a small hat and get your money back."

The two Zanucks keep in close contact, communicating by telephone and teletype several times daily. "In the old days, my father could staff and cast a picture in minutes from the card file listing everyone under contract," Richard Zanuck said. "Nowadays, planning a picture takes longer than making one. Jesus, you spend hours fighting with agents over billing, salary, fringe benefits, start dates, stop dates, the works." He leaned back in his chair and ran his finger across his hairline. "D.Z. doesn't have the temperament for this sort of thing," he said. "His inclination was always to throw an agent out of his office. Not me. I like to wheel and deal."

Several days later, Richard Zanuck asked me to come by his office as he demonstrated his capacity for wheeling and dealing. He was slumped at his desk, picking at his fingernails with a letter opener. With him was Owen McLean, the studio's executive casting director, a heavy-set, round-faced man whose lips are set firmly against his teeth. "Agents always travel in pairs," Zanuck explained, nodding at McLean. "You can't play a lone hand against them. You've got to have someone backing you up, taking notes." His lips parted in a quick smile. "Just in case."

His secretary buzzed and announced that agents Evarts Ziegler and Richard Shepherd were in the outer office. There was a minimum of small talk as the agents entered the office. The project under discussion involved Paul Newman, director Martin Ritt and the husband-wife writing team of Irving Ravetch and Harriet Frank, Jr., the quartet responsible for the hugely successful *Hud.* Their new project was a Western called *Hombre*, the story of a white man who preferred to live among the Indians and who against his will came out into the white man's world. The meeting had certain ritual aspects. The game lay in not yielding a point too easily, in dreaming up new demands just as a detail appeared settled. No one seemed to think it extraordinary that the two agents began by demanding $1.3 million for the four people in the package.

There was no argument over Newman: $750,000 against 10 per cent of the gross until the picture showed a profit. After that, a piece of the profits.

Then the Ravetches. "They get $150,000 a picture," said Ziegler, a smooth, expensively tailored man who doodled constantly with a gold pencil.

Zanuck agreed without comment.

"Irving is going to co-produce," Ziegler said. "That's fifty more."

Zanuck looked up quickly. "It was twenty-five the other day," he said. "You changed the figures."

"Not changed," Ziegler replied. He searched for the proper word. "Corrected."

"No," Zanuck said.

Ziegler doodled a row of zeros on a piece of paper and without looking up said, "Richard Zanuck is being cold to me."

Zanuck shrugged. Ziegler did not argue the point.

The longest discussion was over Ritt. He had once been under contract to Fox and the Studio was now suing him for failure to live up to that contract's provisions. All film companies file charges almost promiscuously, since a lawsuit is a potent bargaining tool in any subsequent negotiations. Few of the suits ever come to trial.

Painfully earnest, with furrowed brow, Shepherd opened for $350,000 for Ritt. Zanuck laughed.

"He's getting $300,000 for his current picture," Shepherd said.

Zanuck picked up the letter opener and laughed again. Shepherd agreed to cut Ritt's price to $250,000, if Fox dropped the lawsuit.

A look of surprise crossed Zanuck's face. "If we drop the suit, he only gets one-fifty," he said. He gnawed at a fingernail. "All my legal people tell me we've got an open and shut case."

"You're putting a price tag on the merits or lack of merits of a piece of litigation," Shepherd protested.

Zanuck smiled. "There's nothing I can do," he said. "If we drop the suit, my legal department is going to lose the prestige of winning a case. That means a lot to a lawyer. I've got to consider that."

They argued back and forth, Shepherd prefacing every remark with "In all honesty . . . I must be truthful . . . In all fairness . . ." His figure dropped slowly and Zanuck's came up. They finally met at $200,000, with Fox agreeing to drop the litigation. Shepherd was still reluctant. "I'll have to check Marty's financial needs for the rest of the year," he said.

When the agents finally left the office, Zanuck picked a piece of paper off his desk and showed it to McLean.

"We'll make a deal," he said. "No doubt about that." The paper was a carbon copy of a memo he had sent Darryl Zanuck in New York several days before, stating that he could tie up Ritt and the rest of the package for exactly what he had just agreed to pay. The deal was confirmed the next day.

2

❝ *I like it better than Frank's,* **❞**

Arthur Jacobs said

By the time I returned to the Studio, *Hombre* had been completed and was in release. (*"Hombre's* 4th Frisco Frame Boff 16G"—*Daily Variety.*) There were forty-eight features in various stages of production, nine television series shooting and a score of others in the planning and pilot stage. Three new sound stages had been built at the main Studio lot in Westwood, bringing the total to twenty-two, but space was still at a premium. Television production had spilled over onto the Studio's secondary lot on Western Avenue, near the Hollywood Freeway, and when all that space was in use, the Studio was forced to rent additional stages from Desilu in Culver City, where two more television shows were shooting. At the Studio's ranch in the San Fernando Valley, *Planet of the Apes*, a science-fiction morality tale about a simian civilization, starring Charlton Heston, was shooting its exteriors, as were two television Westerns, *Custer* and *Daniel Boone*. In the absence of a back lot, every available inch at the Westwood lot was in use. An alley had been converted into an all-purpose French street, the exterior of Sound Stage 5 into the Gotham City Municipal Library for the television show *Batman*, and the outside of the commissary into the Colonial Post Inn in Peyton Place Square.

The trend was up. All twenty-two sound stages on the Westwood lot had been repainted in pastel Mondrian designs. A New Talent Program had been initiated, and every day on Sound Stage 2, the twenty-two young actors and actresses in the school, each paid a minimum of $175 a week, with first six-month and then yearly options on their contracts, underwent a strenuous regimen of dancing and acting lessons. They were given occasional roles in features and television to test their screen presence, were depended upon to attend major premieres, the girls in dresses provided by the Studio's wardrobe department, and were always available for such publicity functions as launching pigeons by the maypole in Century City to open the Southern California Festival of Flowers. There were whirlwind daily tours through the Studio at $2 a head and there was a more elaborate $50 tour for business executives from 500 major American corporations. The $50 tour included a chauffeured limousine to and from the Studio, a personal guide in a red, white and blue miniskirt, a visit to an active sound stage, a test of the dashboard controls on Batman's Batmobile, lunch in the commissary, a look at unedited film in one of the Studio's screening rooms, and a glass of California champagne with the guide at the end of the day.

But the Studio's main concern remained what motion picture people call The Product. In the cutting room, the $18 million production of Dr. Dolittle, a musical fantasy starring Rex Harrison and based on Hugh Lofting's wistful and delicate children's stories, was in the final stages of editing. On the sound stages, Star!, a $12 million musical biography based loosely on the life of Gertrude Lawrence and starring Julie Andrews, was shooting. No cast had been set yet, nor had the script been completed, for Robert Fryer's $4.5 million production of The Boston Strangler. And dominating the Studio was a huge billboard that said: "THINK 20TH."

There were problems with the script of The Boston Strangler. The Studio had purchased the book from author Gerold Frank for $250,000 and assigned it to Robert Fryer to produce. It was Fryer's first motion picture assignment after producing a string of hit Broadway musicals, including Sweet Charity and Mame. A stocky, red-haired man with a delayed, slightly abstracted demeanor, Fryer drove a black Rolls-Royce and, as if resisting the studied casualness of the Studio, he still dressed Eastern—tweed jackets, gray flannel slacks, double-breasted blue suits. The Strangler was supposed to start shooting in the fall, but on the hot midsummer afternoon when I first met Fryer, the script was still incomplete. The first script, by English playwright Terence Rattigan, had not worked out, and Fryer had assigned the job of writing a new script to Edward Anhalt, a veteran Hollywood writer who had won Academy Awards for *Panic in the Streets* and for *Becket.* One of the highest paid writers in Hollywood, Anhalt works entirely on his boat and had driven onto the lot that afternoon only to report his progress to Fryer and Richard Fleischer, who was going to direct *The Strangler.* The meeting took place in Fleischer's office in the ramshackle, barracks-like Old Writers Building.

"Well?" Fryer said, sinking into a chair and loosening his striped tie.

"We're not going to make it," Fleischer said pleasantly. He is a quiet, infinitely patient man in his early fifties. His father, Max Fleischer, was a pioneer in the animated cartoon field, a guiding hand behind *Popeye* and *Betty Boop.* The younger Fleischer directed Richard Zanuck's first feature film, *Compulsion,* and had been employed steadily at the Studio ever since Richard Zanuck had taken over as production chief. He had just finished directing *Dr. Dolittle,* and besides *The Boston Strangler* he was also preparing to co-direct *Tora, Tora, Tora,* an account of the Japanese attack on Pearl Harbor.

"I need a Fresca," Fryer said. The air conditioner was on full, but there were beads of sweat on his forehead. "What am I going to tell Dick Zanuck?"

"That we're not going to go to Boston in September," Fleischer said. He knotted a loose thread around a button on his jacket. "There's no point in going if the script isn't finished."

Fryer looked across the table at Anhalt. He seemed to be controlling his anxiety with great physical effort. "When are you going to be finished, Eddie?"

Anhalt neatly arranged a pile of file cards on the coffee table. He was wearing Ben Franklin half-glasses, a turtleneck sweater and a tailored summer-weight hacking jacket. He has a rugged outdoor face, his head is completely shaved and he looks fifteen years younger than his fifty-five years.

"The first of November," Anhalt said finally.

Fryer sighed. "Can't we send a second unit to Boston in September?"

"Why?" Fleischer said.

"To shoot exteriors," Fryer said hesitantly.

"You've got a problem," Fleischer said. He thought for a moment. "Two problems. You don't have a finished script, you might add locations, you might drop locations. Then you send actors to Boston—I'm not talking about the principals—you're not sure they'll still be available when principal photography starts."

Fryer looked at Anhalt for support, but Anhalt only shook his head. "I say we can't start with half a script," he said. He riffled through his cards. "We've got sixty people in the first forty pages and they're all speaking parts. A lot of those are going to be cut and boiled down and collapsed, so you can't really cast."

"But if we send a second unit, we can get the full feeling of the fall," Fryer insisted. "We don't start shooting until January, we've got a winter picture. You get a late spring in Boston. It doesn't get warm until May. We want the change of seasons. Otherwise . . ." His voice trailed off. "Otherwise we get a winter picture."

Anhalt peered over his half-glasses at Fleischer. "You can use a sundial to show the change of seasons."

A slow smile flickered across Fleischer's face. "How about the pages falling off a calendar?" he said. "Or maybe leaves dropping off a tree in full bloom."

"You must think you're David Lean," Anhalt said.

"Listen . . ." Fryer began. "Dick, listen."

"Look, Bob," Fleischer said quietly. "I can't see how we can possibly be ready to start principal photography in November." He pointed to Anhalt's file cards. "Unless we put sprocket holes in those cards and run them through the projector."

The three men looked at one another. Fleischer drummed his fingers on the arm of his chair. "Now the question is, what do we tell Dick Zanuck? If we can't make November 1, when do we go?"

"The first of January?" Fryer said. With his finger, he removed the sweat from his brow. "I mean, is that a reasonable time?"

Fleischer folded his arms and glanced at Anhalt. "Okay," Anhalt said.

The postponement of *The Boston Strangler* upset the delicate balance of the Studio's feature scheduling. Several weeks before, Richard Zanuck had also dropped *The Nine Tiger Man* from the Fox schedule. The Studio had spent months trying to work out a reasonable budget for the picture, which was to be based on Lesley Blanch's novel, to be directed by George Cukor, and to star Robert Shaw. "The *Nine Tiger Man* budget started at eleven million, we hacked it to eight, then chopped it down to seven-two," Zanuck said one morning a few days after Fryer's meeting on *The Boston Strangler*. "The sets would have cost a million, the costumes five or six hundred thousand. You've got to wonder if Bob Shaw can carry that kind of money. I would have gambled on six, but even that would have been a gamble."

Zanuck wiped a speck of dust off a bronzed baby

shoe behind his desk. Though *The Nine Tiger Man* had been scrubbed, the Studio still had a commitment with Shaw to do a picture for $300,000. One possibility was for Shaw to play the title role in *The Boston Strangler*. Another was for the English actor to star in a film based on Iris Murdoch's novel, *The Severed Head*. A package for *The Severed Head* had been offered to the Studio, which included Shaw, French actress Anouk Aimee, producers Elliot Kastner and Jerry Gershwin, and screenwriter Frederic Raphael, who won an Academy Award for his original screenplay, *Darling*. Zanuck was less than sanguine about the box office possibilities of *The Severed Head*. He thought the property too intellectual for the budget involved and just that morning had expressed his doubts over the telephone to Freddie Fields, president of Creative Management Associates, the agency involved in packaging the project.

Zanuck's secretary brought in some letters for him to sign. He read them quickly, then flicked on his intercom.

"Yes, Dick."

"Can you come in?" Zanuck said.

A moment later, David Brown popped in the back door of Zanuck's office. Brown is a handsome, gray-haired man in his middle fifties, the husband of Helen Gurley Brown, author of *Sex and the Single Girl* and editor of *Cosmopolitan* magazine. He had been the head of the Studio's story department for years, then had left to go into publishing as editorial director of New American Library. He had subsequently returned to Fox as vice president of story operations, and was now, after the Zanucks, the most important man in the production end of the Studio. His headquarters are in New York, but he divides his time between his New York office, Los Angeles and Europe. With the Zanucks, he passes on every important property acquisition and is in on all major packaging, casting, budgeting and scheduling decisions. He is bland and slightly vague, except when talking to either Zanuck.

"Yes, Dick," Brown said. He pulled out a pipe and blew through the stem.

"It looks like we won't be able to start *The Strangler* until the week after New Year's," Zanuck said.

"What's that do with Bob Shaw?" Brown asked.

"He's intrigued with the idea, but he won't comment until after he sees some pages."

A billow of smoke rose from Brown's pipe. "When will we have a script?"

"Fryer says November 1st."

"A long time to keep him waiting," Brown said. He puffed on his pipe. "Can we lay off *Severed Head* on Metro?"

"I talked to Freddie Fields and he's working on it," Zanuck said. "He says it can be made for one-eight. I think we're in for two-five minimum."

"Minimum," Brown said. He took a pencil and wrote some figures on a scratch pad. "$300,000 for Shaw, $150,000 for Aimee, $210,000 for Raphael, $100,000 for the producers—that's almost $800,000 above the line and that doesn't include a director. What's the director laid in for?"

"$75,000," Zanuck said.

"You'll never get anyone for that," Brown said. "It's too low."

Zanuck nodded. "For anyone good."

"How about Michael Winner?"

"He's one-fifty after *The Jokers.*"

Brown watched Zanuck carefully. "It's a marginal property," he said finally. "No question, we'd jump at it for one-six."

"With overhead," Zanuck said.

"With overhead," Brown echoed.

Zanuck leaned back in his chair. "Let's drop it then," he said with finality. "One more thing. Larry Turman said that Joe Levine was interested in *In the Spring the War Ended.*" Turman was a young producer under a non-exclusive contract to Fox. He had brought the novel by Steven Linakis to the Studio, which had spent several hundred thousand dollars developing a screenplay before deciding not to go ahead with the project. "I told him we put $280,000 into it, all told, and that if he could lay it off on Levine, we'd settle for fifty cents on the dollar."

"Fine, Dick," David Brown said.

Star! was shooting on Sound Stage 14, and a day or so later I walked onto the set as director Robert Wise was setting up a shot. A onetime film editor who worked with Orson Welles on *Citizen Kane,* Wise won Academy Awards for his direction of *West Side Story* and *The Sound of Music.* He was sitting high up on a camera crane, shouting instructions through a salmon and gray bullhorn. The shot was a studio pickup of a double-decked London bus carrying revelers to a party given by Julie Andrews, who was playing Gertrude Lawrence. The first part of the sequence had been shot on location in a mews in London, the last in a park in New York. The intermediate segment, now being set up, was a matte shot of the bus rolling toward its ultimate destination in the park. Behind the bus was a giant blue screen on which later would be projected the English countryside passing by, thus giving the illusion that the bus was actually moving.

The scene was number 79 and the script directions read:

UPPER DECK—NIGHT (PROCESS)
Here also the guests are undoing their presents. Tony stands at the front of the upper deck blowing a loud and joyful "View Halloo" on a long hunting horn.

On the side of the vintage red bus was written "London General Omnibus Company, Limited, John Christopher Mitchell, Secretary & Treasurer," as well as an itinerary— "Bank—Ludgate Circus—Strand—Victoria Station—Walham Green—Hammersmith." The bus was on a hydraulic jack, and on either side stagehands were rocking it gently with two-by-fours pried underneath to give a semblance of motion. High up in the rafters, another stagehand slowly waved a prop tree branch in front of a light onto a screen so that the shadow of passing shrubbery could be seen reflected in the bus's windows. The shot took in only the upper deck, so that the bottom was empty. The principals and extras were all dressed in evening clothes, white tie for the men, period 1920's dresses for the women.

On the crane, Wise peered through the camera, composing the shot, his hands expertly working the flywheels. When he was satisfied, he picked up the bullhorn. "All right, let's have a rehearsal," he shouted. "I want a lot of brouhaha. This is the 1920's and you're all a little high. I think some of you might have been a little high before, so you need no instructions from me."

The actors laughed and began to shout and move around the top of the bus. The stagehands rocked the vehicle.

"That's it, that's it," Wise said. "Slurp a little champagne. Blow your horn, Michael." Michael Craig, an English actor who was playing the Horse Guards officer who was Gertrude Lawrence's lover, raised the hunting horn to his lips and began to blow it drunkenly. There was no sound; the sound would be dubbed in later. "That's okay, that's nice, more where that came from," Wise said. "Okay."

Wise took his bullhorn once again. He told Craig to keep blowing his horn a few seconds longer and asked Daniel Massey, another English actor who was playing Noel Coward, to come in faster on his line. "You're waiting too long, Dan. There's other actors with dialogue in this scene and they're waiting on your cue." He looked through the camera again. "Okay, let's take a picture."

The actors returned to their places. The buzzer was sounded and the set doors were locked. The slate boy wrote "Scene 79, Take 1" on his board and snapped it in front of the camera. The assistant director, Reggie Callow, a bulbous, apoplectic-looking man, called for quiet. "Ac-tion," Wise said.

The camera started to roll. Almost immediately Wise called "Cut." Impatiently he shouted down to Callow. "Reggie, what's the matter with the blue screen? There's a shadow over there on the right."

Callow dispatched an electrician to look at the blue screen. Seconds later the electrician reported that a light had burned out behind the screen causing the shadow.

"Goddamn it, that's the second time this morning," Callow bellowed. "Fix the goddamn thing."

Wise climbed down from his perch. He was nervously jiggling a handful of coins. "This is what makes picture making tedious," he said, settling into a leather director's chair on the back of which was written "Robert Wise." I asked how long he had been working on the film. "Three years," he said. His eyes moved slowly around the set, taking in everything. "I didn't really want to do another big picture," he said. "Period pictures take so damn much time. For *The Sand Pebbles*" —Wise's last picture for Fox, a $12 million story about the U. S. Navy in China during the 1920's—"we had to build our own junks and our own rickshas. The ones they had in Hong Kong and Taiwan weren't period." He shifted the coins from his left to his right hand. "I want to do something where I don't have to take down television antennas in order to shoot. A nice simple picture where the people wear their own clothes and I can shoot the TV aerials." He pushed his hand through his graying hair. "But who knows. There was a picture of mine on TV the other night—*The Haunting*—a nice small picture that didn't make a dime. Then I made one with Harry Belafonte, *Odds Against Tomorrow*, again a nice small picture, and it dropped out of sight." The coins went back into his pocket. "So I guess I'm stuck with the big ones."

The light was finally fixed and Wise climbed back up onto the crane. The script called for Julie Andrews to say, "Open your presents, everyone," but because she was not included in the shot, she was not on the set. "Okay," Wise said through his bullhorn. "I'll say Julie's line and everyone look toward the back of the bus. This is a take, not a rehearsal, so everyone open the presents. Don't throw the paper out of the bus, please," he explained patiently, as if talking to a child. "Just put it on the floor."

Callow called for quiet and the red shooting light began to flash on the stage door. As the bus rocked on its jack, the actors bustled about on the upper deck, opening the presents. Each box contained a bathing suit for the swimming party they were on their way to attend.

"Cut," Wise said, when the shot was completed. "That was nice, very nice. Let's print it."

On the bus, an actress stood up and waved at Wise. "Are we supposed to get the same suits we wear at the party?" she said.

"Yes, dear," Wise said.

"But I was fitted for a green one and this is a blue one."

"Son of a bitch," Callow said.

A resigned look flickered across Wise's face. The swim suits were rewrapped and sorted out so that each actor got the bathing suit for which he had been fitted. It was nearly an hour before the scene was ready to be reshot. The actors milled around the stage. Some read *The Hollywood Reporter* and *Daily Variety* and others talked and drank coffee.

"Don't spill any goddamn coffee on those costumes," Callow bawled.

After a half dozen takes, the shot was finally printed. The lights came on and the camera was shifted for the next bus setup. The scene called for the women to go to the bottom of the bus and the men to stay on the upper deck and change into their bathing suits. Wise did not move from the crane. He told Callow to have the electrician check the lights behind the blue screen once again. The shot was finally set up. The buzzer sounded and the actors on the top of the bus began to undress. Suddenly Wise called, "Cut."

"Gentlemen," he said quietly, "this is a period picture. If men wore GI T-shirts during the 1920's, nobody has bothered to inform me about it. And so I can only assume that no one wore GI T-shirts during the 1920's. Now is anyone wearing an old-style undershirt, the kind with shoulder straps?"

Several actors on the top of the bus raised their hands.

"All right, then you people can take off your shirts," Wise said. His patience was beginning to wear thin. "The rest of you fake it. Just fool with your buttons until I get the shot."

"I'm not wearing anything underneath," Michael Craig said.

"Then you can take off your shirt, too," Wise said. He lingered deliberately over each word. "But *only* . . . the actors not wearing anything or who've got those old-style undershirts I want to take off their shirts." He paused. "Are we ready, gentlemen? I'd like to get this shot in before lunch."

The following afternoon, Richard Zanuck had an appointment to see Phil Gersh, an agent who looks like a successful former light heavyweight champion and who represents both Wise and Richard Fleischer. Gersh had no specific reason to see Zanuck, but was merely sounding out the Studio's intentions toward his clients when their current assignments expired.

"You ever read *Candy*, Dick?" he said as he sat down.

"Jesus, Phil. You're not peddling that one?"

"Well, you know." Gersh shrugged. "There's two new writers on it, Waterhouse and Hall, you know, those English guys. They got a new approach. Nothing pornographic. It's real cute, in fact."

Zanuck was noncommittal. "I'd want to see a script, Phil."

"Oh, I understand that, Dick. You can't have that dame balling everyone on camera."

Zanuck smiled. He took an ashtray off his desk and brushed some ashes into it.

"Listen," Gersh said. "You got anything for Bob Wise after *Star!*?"

"I've been laying off him," Zanuck said. "He says he wants a long rest."

"He says he wants to do a little picture, too," Gersh said. "I wouldn't lay off him too much. There's a lot of action on the outside and he's listening to it."

"I'll keep that in mind," Zanuck said.

"He likes it here, he wants to stay, I want you to know that," Gersh said. "But I got to tell you he's listening to all this activity."

"I'll give it a thought," Zanuck said.

Gersh rose and shook Zanuck's hand. "That's all I ask, Dick," he said. "We'll talk."

"The problems we had with *Dolittle*," Arthur P. Jacobs said. "I mean the *problems*." The producer of *Dr. Dolittle* lit a slim dark Sherman cigarettello and dropped the match into a wastebasket, looking for a moment to see that the basket did not burst into flames. He buzzed his secretary and asked her to bring him in a plate of Triscuits and a diet soda. A trim former press agent with a slack chin and dark, darting eyes, he had recently recovered from a heart attack and was on a diet. He had lost thirty pounds, given up bread and butter and was now drinking only diet soda. The air conditioner in his office in the Apjac bungalow—the name of Jacobs' production company is an anagram based on his first two initials and the first three letters in his last name—was turned up so high that the temperature seemed almost polar. "I mean," he said, "if I knew we were in for these kind of problems at the beginning, I never would have done it."

Dr. Dolittle was only Jacobs' second picture. He had made his first, *What A Way to Go!*, six years before and had spent most of the intervening years trying to put *Dolittle* together. His first problem was getting the estate of Hugh Lofting to release title of the books for a motion picture. For years, the Lofting estate had turned down every effort to film the *Dolittle* stories. A born promoter, Jacobs had interested Rex Harrison and Alan Jay Lerner, the librettist and lyricist of *My Fair Lady,* in the project and with these names was given the go-ahead by the Lofting estate. "So I got Lerner," Jacobs said, munching on a Triscuit. "He worked on the picture fifteen months on and off, mostly off. We painted an office for him, painted his name on a parking space, and then we waited. And waited some more. I get him on the phone, he tells me he knows what he wants, it's all in his head. More phone calls. He tells me he wants to see me here, I go see him, he tells me he's leaving for New York in ten minutes. I make an appointment to go see him in New York, I go to New York, they tell me he's in Rome. That's it. So I signed Leslie Bricusse to write the script and do the score."

The signing of Bricusse created another problem, this one with Harrison. A young English writer who had co-authored the Broadway hit, *Stop the World, I Want To Get Off*, Bricusse was an unknown quantity to Harrison, and Harrison preferred working only with people he knew. But after hearing several of Bricusse's songs and seeing a portion of his script, Harrison agreed to continue. The question now was who was going to direct the picture. The three biggest names bruited about were John Huston, William Wyler and Vincente Minnelli, each an Academy Award winner. "Darryl wanted Huston," Jacobs said, "but I figured there was already enough temperament with Rex without getting Huston involved. Minnelli was old-fashioned and Wyler would take fifty takes of every shot and the picture would end up costing thirty-five million. Who else was there? Dick Zanuck liked Fleischer ever since *Compulsion*, so I said okay. Now we had to persuade Rex, so Fleischer and I fly to his home in Portofino and I sort of indicated to him that if he didn't want Fleischer, maybe we could get along without him. We spent a nice weekend, and at the end, Rex gets me alone to talk about Fleischer. 'Nice chap, good chap,' he says, and that was that."

Jacobs leaned across his desk. "So now Rex had a contract, he was getting more money than God, we were in business," he said. "Then Rex says, 'Good-by,

sue me, I'm not going to do it.' " Jacobs shuddered the-
atrically. "We have a picture called *Dr. Dolittle*, twelve
million going in, and no one to play Dr. Dolittle. We
scratch around and come up with Christopher Plummer. The studio liked him, he'd been in *The Sound of
Music*, but it was no secret we were in a jam and we
had to lay out $300,000 to get him. So Fox wires Rex,
something like, 'As per your request, you have been re-
lieved of your *Dr. Dolittle* assignment and replaced by
another artist.' Next day his agents call, Rex didn't
mean it, he just wanted a few changes, and so on and
so forth. So we pay off Plummer, he's got us over a barrel with a nice legal contract. But Rex is back and we're
ready to go."

Dr. Dolittle actually began shooting in England in
late June, 1966, with Harrison, Samantha Eggar, Anthony Newley and Richard Attenborough in the leading
roles. In fifty-eight days of shooting in England, only
five were rainless. Most of the English locations were in
a classic little Wiltshire village called Castle Combe.
Fleischer had obtained all the necessary permissions
for widening and damming a small river nearby, turning Castle Combe into the tiny seaport of Puddleby-on-
the-Marsh, where Dr. Dolittle lived. (He had also built
a community television antenna, so that he could remove anachronistic TV aerials from Castle Combe's
cottages.) The first morning of shooting, two young
Englishmen, objecting to Hollywood's transformation
of the village, tried to blow up the dam. This set the
tone for relations between Castle Combe and the *Dolittle* company for the rest of its stay in England.

Another problem was the training of the animals befriended by Dr. Dolittle. Months before shooting began, hundreds of animals had been selected for training at Jungleland in Thousand Oaks, California. Because of the strict quarantine laws in the United Kingdom, two sets of animals had to be trained, one for shooting in Hollywood, the other for shooting in England. All the principal animals in the cast—Jip the Dog, Polynesia the Parrot, Chee-Chee the Chimpanzee, Sophie the Seal and Gub-Gub the Pig—had doubles. Pigs grow so rapidly that Jacobs had to replace Gub-Gub every month with a new and properly sized porker, and both Chee-Chee and Jip had not one but three backups. Simulating sound-stage conditions, the trainers at Jungleland constantly flashed lights at the animals and moved among them so that they would not get skittish when finally confronted with the high-powered arcs and the hundreds of people present on a set. Six months were devoted to teaching Chee-Chee the Chimpanzee how to cook bacon and eggs. On Stage 20 at the Studio, Dr. Dolittle's study was constructed in anticipation of the fact that few of the animals were housebroken. The floor was slightly tilted and fitted with a drain so that it might be hosed off easily. In all, Jacobs spent $1 million simply to train, house, feed and transport the animals.

Jacobs seemed relatively unconcerned that the delays and the problems had run Dolittle up to nearly $18 million, or approximately $6 million over budget. "Everyone wants to be identified with this picture," he said. "*Everyone*. All the big companies, they want to do some kind of tie-in promotion. You won't be able to go into a store without seeing Dr. Dolittle advertising something.

You got to figure that's going to bring people into the theater. I mean, these are big companies. They don't do this just for *any* picture."

Saying it seemed to reassure him further, and he walked out into the anteroom of his office in buoyant spirits. "Who's got the keys to my car?" he asked. He had just bought a new Dual Ghia, one of Hollywood's most favored automobiles. "I sent them out to get another set made."

A secretary handed him the keys. "You ought to get a gold one," she said.

"They send you one," Jacobs said. "They really do."

He examined himself quickly in a mirror and walked outside. The Dual Ghia was parked in his space outside the bungalow. Jacobs circled the car. "Someone left a fingerprint on the windshield," he said. He buffed it off with the sleeve of his black alpaca sweater and then stepped back and studied the automobile.

"I like it better than Frank's," he said finally.

"Frank who?" the secretary said.

Jacobs looked pained. "Sinatra," he said.

3

"You'll get the music lovers,

no doubt about that, none at all,"

Richard Zanuck said

Several days later, Arthur Jacobs sent me a preliminary list of the companies with licensing arrangements with the Studio for tie-in advertising and promotion on *Dr. Dolittle.* There were approximately fifty licensees who would spend $12 million on consumer advertising featuring the picture. The Studio was making arrangements for *Dolittle* displays in 10,000 retail stores throughout the country, a food company had ordered 20,000 eight-foot displays featuring Rex Harrison, and another food company had 15,000 Harrison displays. A soft-drink company was introducing "Dr. Dolittle Chocolate Soda" and a national bakery concern a special box of animal crackers featuring all the animals used in the picture. Over 200 million cereal boxes were being distributed with allied *Dolittle* promotion. In all, some 300 items, with an estimated retail value of $200 million, were involved in the promotion. Among the items were pet foods, cereals, a Dolittle medicine kit, a Dolittle hat, a Pushmi-Pullyu toy, a television record player for children, a Polynesia doll, clocks and watches, a singing doll, knitted T-shirts, greeting cards, sweatshirts, children's card game sets, children's luggage, pencil boxes, plastic inflatable toys, novelty hats, balloons, wrist watches, combs, brushes, sunglasses, place mats, ceramic ware, notebooks, tumblers, billfolds, change purses, color slides and viewers, night lights, toy musical instruments, yo-yos, flashlight novelty items, board games, model kits, jigsaw puzzles, novelty savings banks, storybooks, activity books, buttons, play money, children's coloring books, doctors' kits, nurses' kits, animal toys, children's schoolbags, lunch kits, puppets, charm bracelets, scrapbooks, diaries, robes, coloring sets, sewing sets, 3D film cards, magic slates and costumes.

Mary Ann McGowan, Richard Zanuck's secretary, came into his office and announced that director Henry Koster, producer Robert Buckner and three William Morris agents were waiting outside.

"What's Buckner's first name?" Zanuck asked.

"Robert," Mary Ann McGowan said, as she disappeared out the door. "They call him Bob."

The five visitors filed into Zanuck's office. Zanuck rose and shook the hand of each. "Hello, Bob," he said to Buckner.

Koster, Buckner and two of the agents arranged themselves in chairs in front of Zanuck's desk. The third agent slid onto a couch in the corner of the office. Koster cleared his throat and wiped his forehead with a handkerchief. He is a portly man with thinning hair slicked down on the top of his head and a thick middle-European accent. At one time he had directed a number of pictures for the Studio. "I have a story for you, Dick," he said.

Zanuck nodded. No one spoke for a moment. Koster wiped his forehead again and mashed the handkerchief in his hand.

"I have wanted to bring to the screen a story of great music," he said, "ever since I first came to this country and made *A Hundred Men and a Girl*." He looked to Zanuck for encouragement. "With Deanna Durbin," he added.

Zanuck picked up the bronzed baby shoe behind his desk and began to turn it around in his hands. His eyes did not catch Koster's.

"We fade in on Moscow," Koster said. "Behind the credits, we hear one of the world's great symphony orchestras playing—Shostakovich would be good for Moscow. The orchestra has a flamboyant, tempestuous conductor—I think Lenny Bernstein will love this idea. As we finish the credits, we come on on the orchestra and then we close on the cymbals. It is obvious that the cymbal player is sick. The orchestra is supposed to leave Moscow that night for a charity concert in New York." Koster paused for effect. He was sweating profusely. "For crippled children."

One of the Morris agents was examining his fingernails. The head of the agent on the couch began to nod.

"When the concert is over, we find that the cymbal player has a contagious disease," Koster said. He wound the handkerchief around his palms. "We can work out the disease later. The orchestra must be quarantined in Moscow. All except the Lenny Bernstein character. I think we can work out that he had the right shots. Anyway we can get Lenny out of Moscow and back to New York. Now here is your problem, Dick. The charity concert must be canceled."

The agent on the couch had now fallen asleep. An abortive snore jolted him awake.

"Unless," Koster continued. He smiled benignly. "There is a youth orchestra in New York and they can take the place of the symphony at the concert. We have, of course, tried to get the Philadelphia and the Cleveland and Ormandy and George Szell would love to do it, but they have commitments. So the Lenny Bernstein character goes to hear the youth symphony and he says, 'No, I cannot conduct them, they are not good enough.' He will not yield, the concert must be canceled, there will be no money for the crippled children." Koster's voice softened. "But then the president of the charity comes to plead with him against cancellation." Koster's head swiveled around, taking in everyone in the room. "In his arms, he is carrying a small boy—with braces on his legs."

Buckner seemed to sense that Zanuck's attention was wavering. "We have a love story, too, Dick," he said.

Koster picked up the cue. "Yes, we have a love story," he said. "There is a beautiful Chinese cellist who does not speak a word of English and a beatnik kook who plays the violin." The words rolled over his tongue. "They communicate through the international language of music."

"Don't forget the jazz," Buckner said.

"We can get jazz into our story, Dick," Koster said. "You see, the concert is only five days away and there are not enough players in the youth orchestra, so the conductor—the Lenny Bernstein character—goes out and hunts them up in a bunch of weird joints."

"Jazz joints," Buckner said.

The top of Koster's head was slick with perspiration. His voice began to quicken. "Working day and night, the conductor molds these untutored players into a symphony orchestra. In just five days." Koster's face grew somber. "Then we get word from Moscow. The quarantine has been lifted. The orchestra can get back to New York in time for the concert."

Zanuck gazed evenly, unblinkingly at Koster.

"Here is the crux of our story, Dick," Koster said. "Will our conductor use the youth symphony, or will he use his own orchestra, thus destroying by his lack of faith this beautiful instrument"—Koster's hands moved up and down slowly—"he has created in just five days?"

Koster sighed and leaned back, gripping both the arms on his chair. There was silence in the office. Zanuck cleared his throat.

"Very nicely worked out," he said carefully. "Very nicely." His jaw muscles began to work as he considered his thoughts. "But I'm afraid it's not for us at the moment." He squared the bronzed baby shoe against the edge of his desk. "We've got a lot of musical things on the schedule right now—*The Sound of Music* is still doing great business, just great, we've got *Dr. Dolittle* and we're working on *Hello, Dolly!*—and I don't think we should take on another." He paused, seeking the right words. "And quite frankly, I'm just a little afraid of this kind of music. "You'll get the music lovers, no doubt about that, none at all. But how about the Beatle fans?"

Koster made a perfunctory objection, but the meeting was over. As if on cue, the dozing agent awoke, and after an exchange of small talk, agents and clients departed Zanuck's office, hurling pleasantries over their shoulders. For a long time, Zanuck sat chewing on a fingernail, saying nothing.

"Jesus," he said finally.

"You've got to be careful about musicals," David Brown said. "They're very soft in the foreign market. In the old days, you didn't have to consider that much. But you do now. We get over fifty per cent of our rentals abroad. You take a massive hit like *Sound of Music.* Even there two-thirds to three-quarters of the rentals have come from the English-speaking world. In some foreign markets, they take a musical and want to cut the music. That's why we didn't bid on *Fiddler on the Roof.* It's a lovely show, we were all agreed on that. But we thought it would be very soft in the provinces."

Brown ran a pipe cleaner through the stem of his pipe. On his desk was a script from Ruth Gordon, the actress-playwright wife of playwright Garson Kanin. The script was scheduled for a Broadway production and had been submitted to the Studio for a possible pre-production film deal. Brown fingered the script delicately and then asked his secretary to get Kanin on the telephone.

"How are you, Gar? . . . Fine . . . And Ruth? . . . Fine . . . Gar, I read Ruth's play and I think it's delightful and fabulous as a play. But it worries me as a picture, Gar. You know fifty-five per cent of our revenues come from abroad and I'm just not sure how something delightful and delicate as this will go over outside this country. It's absurd and it kills us, but that's how it is. But many thanks, Gar, for letting us see it and I'm sure Ruth's going to have a big hit in New York."

Brown hung up the phone and dabbed at his chin. He had cut himself shaving that morning and the tiny piece of toilet paper on his chin was not stanching the blood. He rang for his secretary.

"Could you call the dispensary and have a messenger send me over a Band-aid?" Brown said. He touched his chin again. "On second thought, make it two Band-aids."

Our town's most written-about "A" hostess had better realize that there are not only "A" and "B" parties, but "A" and "B" members of the press. She's been associating indiscriminately with members of the media. And she may just blow her international status.

Joyce Haber, The Los Angeles Times

One morning during the second week of July, when the temperature stood at 97 degrees and the Los Angeles basin lay somnolent in the yellow haze, the Studio landscaping department began stripping the trees in Peyton Place Square, outside the commissary, of their autumn foliage. Late that morning, just before the various offices broke for lunch, the prop department scattered the first artificial snows of winter onto the Peyton Place Green. On the steps of the commissary, Robert Fryer stopped for a moment to watch. "It looks like New England in the winter, doesn't it?" he said to John Bottomly, a tall angular Bostonian who was on a brief flying trip to California.

Bottomly took off his sunglasses and surveyed the scene. "Not really," he said slowly.

Bottomly was the assistant attorney general of Massachusetts who had coordinated the investigation into the Boston Strangler's thirteen sex murders. It was to Bottomly that Albert DeSalvo, the alleged slayer of the thirteen women, had confessed. After the role of DeSalvo, that of Bottomly was the most important in Edward Anhalt's script, and Fryer had hired the Boston attorney, who was now back in private practice, as *The Boston Strangler*'s technical advisor.

Anhalt was waiting for Fryer and Bottomly in the producers' dining room, an executive enclave off the barn-like main room in the commissary. Bottomly hung his jacket over the back of his chair and began to fan himself with the menu.

"We've got a nice *Valley of the Dolls* Salad," the waitress said.

Bottomly stared at the waitress and then at the menu. "*A Guide to the Married Man* Casserole," he read. "*Flim Flam Man* Hamburger, *Two for the Road* Fruit Salad." He looked across the table at Fryer. "I don't see a *Boston Strangler* dish."

"We haven't started shooting," Fryer said. He looked nonplussed.

"New England seafood dinner à la *Boston Strangler*," Bottomly said. He resumed fanning himself. "You know, the police work on the Strangler was really pretty bad. They never checked to see if there was any semen in the mouth of the first six or seven victims. The thing about most murders is if you don't catch the guy right away, chances are he's going to get away."

"I wonder if we're going to run into trouble with this script," Anhalt said. "I mean, it's very clinical. We're dealing with penis and vagina and semen with every murder."

"You take out the semen, you don't have a script," Bottomly said. He scooped a piece of melon. "You know they've got a process now where they can match semen with blood types. They can use it on rape cases if they get it early enough."

Anhalt looked down at his steak sandwich. "Jesus," he said.

"We've got a new problem," Fryer said. "DeSalvo's wife. Irmgard's holding us up on the release."

"How much does she want?" Anhalt said.

"$35,000," Fryer said.

Anhalt gave a short laugh. "Being a wife comes high these days."

"Maybe we can do without her," Fryer said.

"Not if we're going to show Albert the family man," Anhalt said. "She's in two sequences. We've got to show the contrast between Albert at home and Albert getting his rocks off. But $35,000 is ridiculous."

Fryer smiled wanly. "Maybe we can change her name."

"Sure," Anhalt said. "And call DeSalvo Albert Smith?"

"It was just a try," Fryer said. "There's nothing derogatory about her in the script, is there?"

"No, she's just Albert's wife," Anhalt said.

"In the book, in his confession, Albert said she turned him off," Fryer said.

"Jesus," Anhalt said, "I think the script's already complicated enough sexually without throwing that in."

Bottomly reached back into his jacket and pulled out a letter. It was from Irmgard DeSalvo. In the letter, DeSalvo's wife expressed her distaste for *The Boston Strangler* book and said that if either she or her children were portrayed in the film, she would be forced to take legal action.

Fryer pursed his lips. "That's all we need," he sighed. He pushed his plate away and buried his face in his hands.

"She'll give a release," Bottomly said quietly. "It's just a matter of coming up with the right money."

"Christ," Anhalt said. "She sounds like an agent. The letter's just a ploy."

"Exactly," Bottomly said. "I had to track her down halfway around the world. She's changed her name a couple of times. She's remarried. *And* she's pregnant. Give her the right money and she won't cause any trouble."

"What about the kids?" Anhalt said.

"I'd like to see Albert's waiver on that," Bottomly said. "He's not their legal guardian any more, of course, but I would like to see his waiver."

Fryer brightened. "It's over at the William Morris

office." He beckoned the waitress and asked for another glass of iced tea. "I saw Hank Fonda last night," he said. "I think we can get him to play you."

Bottomly brooded for a moment. "What about Gregory Peck? He's the one who really looks like me."

Fryer shook his head. "Not a chance," he said.

Bottomly looked outside the producers' dining room at the mural of Darryl Zanuck glaring down from the wall in the main room. "Darryl Zanuck lives," he said. He kept staring at the mural, transfixed. "His eyes follow you around. They actually follow you around." He shuddered and came back into the conversation. "What about Albert?" he said. "Any ideas about who to play him?"

"Everyone in town wants to," Fryer said. "We even got some pictures from Tony Curtis. He went out and got himself made up like the Strangler and had pictures taken."

Bottomly did not seem impressed. "How about Stuart Whitman?"

"Uh uh," Fryer said. "Dick Fleischer won't work with him." He threw his napkin on the table. "And we've got to keep our director happy."

Richard Fleischer was also scheduled to co-direct *Tora, Tora, Tora,* a film based on the events leading up to and including the Japanese attack on Pearl Harbor. The picture was being done from both the American and the Japanese points of view. The American part of the film was being directed by Fleischer, the Japanese, with English subtitles, by Akiro Kurosawa, the director of *Rashomon* and *The Seven Samurai,* his first American picture after years of being regarded as one of the finest directors in the world. Fleischer was leaving for Honolulu the following Sunday with *Tora, Tora, Tora's* producer, Elmo Williams, to meet with Kurosawa and to scout locations. A day or so before they left, I walked over to the art department with Williams to see a storyboard of the first draft script and map sketches of Oahu that he wanted to show Kurosawa. We went into a cubbyhole on the second floor of the art department building. Tacked to the wall, in dramatic sequence, were scores of rough sketches of various scenes in the script —a code room in Washington, a wardroom on a Japanese flagship, Pearl Harbor before the attack, the Japanese planes approaching Oahu. Williams examined each of the sketches and then asked to see the large detail map of Oahu the art department had drawn. An art director put the map on the shelf. Williams took a grease pencil and lightly traced three lines on the overlay—roughly north to south, south to north, and east to west—all converging on Pearl Harbor.

"There's one thing we've got to remember," Williams said. "We've got to keep the audience oriented. The ordinary guy sitting in Chicago, he looks at a map and he says Japan is off to the left and England is off to the right." He tapped the map with the pencil. "Now the Japs attacked in three different directions, the three I've drawn here, but no planes came in from the west, or from the left side of the map. What we've got to do is get our camera angles so that the Jap planes are always flying from left to right and the Americans are shooting back at them from right to left. We can get an angle to show the proper background for accuracy's sake. But we've got to be careful to make that guy in Chicago know that whenever he sees a plane flying from left to right, he's seeing a Jap plane."

Several days later, Arthur Jacobs called and asked if I wanted to see how a picture was promoted. When I arrived at the Apjac bungalow, Jacobs was sitting at his desk, a telephone cradled in his shoulder. Before him was a small file box containing white, yellow and pink file cards. He cupped his hand over the telephone. "White for dictation, yellow for telephone follow-up, pink for projects," he said. "The secretary cleans it out every week. You got to be organized." He spoke back into the telephone. "You want to know my schedule, I'll give you my schedule." He ran a finger down a piece of paper on his desk. "October 2 through October 7, New York, available for meetings and interviews, October 8, fly to London, October 9 through 14, London, available for meetings and interviews, October 15 through 19, Paris, available for meetings and interviews, October 20, fly to New York, October 23 through 26, New York, available for meetings and interviews."

There are twelve buttons on Jacobs' telephone and he pressed one to take another call. The decor in his office is mustard and brown, and on the walls there are gold-framed posters of Paris art gallery shows—Kandinsky, Dufy, and Toulouse-Lautrec. Scattered about the office that day were various still photographs and book jackets of projects in which Apjac was involved—*Planet of the Apes, The Chairman,* an unpublished novel in which Frank Sinatra was interested in appearing, and a script for *Good-bye, Mr. Chips,* a musical version of the James

Hilton story that Jacobs planned to produce at Metro-Goldwyn-Mayer with Gower Champion as director.

"That's right," Jacobs said into the telephone. "I want the sound track album to go to every major newspaper publisher, editor, columnist, you name it. I want a cocktail party for all the disk jockeys in all the major cities when the *Dolittle* album comes out. And I want the Studio field men to give us a semi-monthly report on the status of all the *Dolittle* window displays in every city in their territory."

As Jacobs hung up the phone, Mort Abrahams, Apjac's vice president and associate producer of *Dr. Dolittle*, walked into the office.

"I just talked to Gower," Abrahams said. "I told him the choreographer wanted $2,000 a week and he went right out of his fucking skull. He said to offer him $750 and if he doesn't like it, we'll get someone else."

Jacobs nodded and lit a small dark cigarette. "*Chips, Dolittle*, all we're selling around here is confusion, Mort," he said. He rummaged around his desk and came up with the record jacket of the sound track album of *Dr. Dolittle*, which had just arrived that morning.

"An original pressing of 500,000," Jacobs said. "The biggest in history. Bigger than *Sound of Music*, bigger than *My Fair Lady*, bigger than anything."

"I like it," Abrahams said.

"You better like it," Jacobs said.

Over the intercom, Jacobs' secretary announced that Arnold Maxin was waiting in the outer office. Maxin was the president of the music publishing firm that was handling the *Dolittle* sheet music. He had arrived to discuss with Jacobs and Abrahams how to push the *Dolittle* score in albums, in singles and on television.

"Arnold, baby," Jacobs said when Maxin came into the room. He is a dark, intense-looking man in his forties. "Let's get some lunch."

They walked out into the noonday sun. Maxin had a blue, chauffeur-driven limousine parked in front of the bungalow.

"I like it, Arnold," Abrahams said.

"You like everything today, Mort," Jacobs said. "Let's take the cart." Ever since his heart attack, Jacobs got around the lot in a striped golf cart. It had once been painted pink and white, the motif colors in the *Dr. Dolittle* advertising campaign; now it was yellow and white. "Give your man a half hour for lunch, Arnold."

Jacobs steered the golf cart up through the French street and parked outside the commissary in Peyton Place Square. An extra dressed in a T-shirt and silver facial monster makeup stared at Jacobs as he walked into the commissary. Jacobs stared back and shook his head slightly. He settled into a chair in the executive dining room, took the bread and butter from his place and put it on the table behind him.

"Listen," Jacobs said. "Bobby Darin just flipped. I played the original score for him at a party at my house and he went right out of his skull. He wants to do the whole album."

"Sammy Davis, too," Abrahams said.

"Sammy, too," Jacobs said.

"We're talking to Andy Williams this afternoon and we sent a man down to Florida to see Sinatra," Maxin said. He reached across to the next table and speared the pat of butter Jacobs had put there. "We're not going to have any trouble with albums. Everyone wants to be identified with this picture. All the major artists, Streisand, Frank, all of them. They know about the picture and they're crazy for the songs." He broke a bread stick in two. "They want to be identified with this picture."

"What about singles?" Abrahams said.

"There you've got a problem," Maxin said carefully. "You go to an artist and try to get him to do a single and he says, 'Sure, if I can be first out with it!' You can't give a first to both Tony Bennett and Matt Monro. So they might hold off."

Jacobs cracked a piece of ice between his teeth. "And then there's the problem with Rex," he said.

"Right," Maxin said. "He's not a singer, the songs are tailored to him. They're his songs, they're identified with Rex Harrison."

"Like *My Fair Lady*," Jacobs said.

"Right," Maxin said. "He had a four-year run in that show and the only big single was 'On the Street Where You Live.' And that wasn't his song, you remember. All the others were so identified with him, no one wanted to follow him. It was like coming on after World War III." He considered his salad. "Maybe you won't have so much of a problem with this picture. It's an original score, nobody's heard the music."

"Are your people working on the TV shows?" Abrahams said.

"Yeah," Maxin said. "We got three of our songs on the first Dean Martin show this fall."

"From *Dolittle*?" Abrahams said, surprised.

"No," Maxin said. "From our catalogue."

"We want to get something from *Dolittle* on the first show, though, Arnold," Abrahams said. "That's the one gets all the ballyhoo, all the reviews."

"We'll work on it," Maxin said reassuringly.

"Maybe we should put our own man on it," Jacobs said. His eyes darted back and forth between Maxin and Abrahams.

"No, my man is a specialist in TV shows," Maxin said. "That's all he does, twelve months a year. You get a man, he goes in to see Dean, Dean says, 'We'll see what we can do.' My man will get a listen."

"I'd like to get on more TV shows," Jacobs said. "And get more singles."

"We got Tony Bennett for a single," Maxin said. "Period. The single we've got to push is 'When I Look into Your Eyes.' That's what I call an easy listening song. It's Frank's kind of play." He jabbed his fork at Jacobs. "With this score, you're not going to get the rock-and-roll stations. Forget it. It's the easy listening songs."

They talked for a while about promoting the score through music and record dealers. "You're going to want the big window displays in the major record stores, right?" Maxin said.

"Right," Jacobs said.

"You know you're going to have to pay for those windows?" Maxin said.

Abrahams stared at him incredulously. "What?" he said.

"You heard me," Maxin said. "You get Liberty's double bay in New York and it's going to cost you fifteen hundred bucks. Sam Goody's 49th Street window goes for a thousand, Korvette's twenty-five hundred."

"Twenty-five hundred for Korvette's?" Jacobs said.

"Fifth Avenue," Maxin said. "The quality trade."

"Jesus Christ," Abrahams said.

Maxin seemed surprised at their naïveté. "No money changes hands," he said. "They just want free albums. You want Sam Goody's front window, you give Sam Goody 700 free albums."

"Is it worth it?" Jacobs said. "I want to know how many windows to buy."

"It . . . is . . . worth it," Maxin said deliberately, making a sweeping gesture with his hand. "Listen, how many mobile displays you got?"

"Fifteen hundred," Jacobs said.

"A *minimum* fifteen hundred you should get," Maxin said. "If a store makes a commitment with a mobile, then they're going to push your record." He snapped his fingers at the waitress. "The cantaloupe's a little hard. Bring me some vanilla ice cream." He turned back to Jacobs. "And you should run a contest for your record distributors. The one who gets the best distribution for the record gets a free trip to Paris, say. Write letters to their wives. Say something like, 'If you want that mink stole we're handing out, your husband should do this and this and this.' It gives the guy on the street selling the album a little incentive."

4

❝ *Wet she was a star,* **❞**

Joe Pasternak said

The budget of every motion picture is divided into "above the line" costs—story, writer, producer, director, cast—and "below the line" costs—labor, sets, costumes, makeup, hair styling, optical and special effects. To the final budget of each picture is added a studio overhead charge that runs to approximately 25 per cent of the actual cost. It is a common complaint in Hollywood that the studio overhead subliminally encourages a certain amount of fat in a studio's own below-the-line budget estimates. It is rare that a department head will choose the cheaper of two alternatives, since higher cost means higher overhead and higher profit for the studio. Thus, in a recent picture (which was not made at Fox), the star's costumes, which ran mainly to smocks and housedresses, were budgeted for $15,000; the costume designer, whose first film this was, estimated that she could have bought the same wardrobe retail for, at most, $2,500.

At the Studio, the job of setting the below-the-line costs and policing them once they have been established falls to the production department. Every weekday morning at 11:30, all the department heads meet in the production bungalow to go over the progress of each feature and television film the Studio has either shooting or in preparation. There are approximately thirty people at this daily meeting, representing the Studio's wardrobe, prop, police, electrical, construction, camera, art, makeup and hair-styling departments. The meeting is chaired by the assistant head of the Studio's production department, Louis "Doc" Merman. One morning I walked into the meeting just as Merman was taking his place at the head of the table. Merman looks like an aging, amiable beagle. His hair has thinned into a few strands on the top and he has imposing bags under his eyes. He rapped his glasses on the table and called the meeting to order.

"Jesus, I saw a stinker last night," he said by way of preface. *"The Way West.* A million dollars in story costs. Jesus." He spread the daily call sheet in front of him. "Anybody got the weather report for tomorrow?"

"Sunny all day, Doc," someone answered.

"Okay, that means we don't have to scratch anything on location," Merman said. *"Sweet Ride* starts tomorrow, right? The company leaves the casting corner at 6:30. Is anyone still in that house they're shooting in down at the beach?"

"No, they all moved out, Doc."

"Who's got the keys to the house?" Merman said.

"We got a watchman there twenty-four hours a day, Doc."

"Okay, that takes care of that one," Merman said. "Now, where do we stand on *The Boston Strangler*?"

He went into every picture listed on the call sheets and the special problems with each.

"When's Barbara Parkins going to be free for looping *Valley of the Dolls*?"

"She's got two days off next week, Doc."

"Well, tie her up," Merman said. "We can't let that go any longer. Is *Planet of the Apes* going to be finished at the ranch this week?"

"Should be, Doc."

"Better be," Merman said. "Warner's wants to rent the cornfield out there Monday."

"Jesus, I don't know, Doc. It's all trampled. Those goddamn apes and horses tore the shit out of it. Warner's will have a hell of a time making it ready."

"That's their problem," Merman said. "How we coming on *Star!*?"

"We got the wardrobe for the vaudeville theater scene coming in on Pan Am Flight 2. The customs agent will be looking for it."

"Goddamn thing better get here," Merman said. "We're going to be shooting that."

"And then we've got to redress Gertie's Maida Vale apartment set," the *Star!* production manager continued. "Bob Wise doesn't like it the way it is."

"Oh, good Christ," Merman said, shaking his head. He looked down the table for the chief of the Studio police. Cartier's, the New York jeweler, had lent the

Star! company $200,000 worth of real jewels for Julie Andrews to wear in her incarnation as Gertrude Lawrence. The security for the stones was in the hands of the Studio police.

"Where you keeping that stuff, Chief?" Merman said.

"Wouldn't you like to know, Doc," the Studio police chief said.

"In a paper bag someplace, I bet."

"That's right, Doc," the chief said.

"Jesus, real jewels, as if we didn't have enough problems," Merman said. "The director says it makes the actors feel good and you can photograph that feeling. That's a load of shit. The main thing you got it for is the publicity." He looked at his watch and gathered together his papers. "Okay," he said, rising from his chair. "That's it till tomorrow."

Ran into Jed Harris at a party the other night and he told me this amusing story: the future husband of a fair lady he planned to marry came to him and said, "My fiancée tells me that she is still in love with you. Do you love her?" "I worship her," was Jed's reply. "Then why don't you marry her?" he was asked. "Because I'd rather shoot myself," Jed retorted.

Radie Harris, The Hollywood Reporter

The Sweet Ride was Joe Pasternak's 105th motion picture and his first for Fox after being under contract to M-G-M for more than twenty-five years. Born in Hungary, he had produced films in Berlin, Vienna and Budapest before arriving in Hollywood in 1937 as producer of *Three Smart Girls, A Hundred Men and a*

Girl and *Mad About Music*. During his quarter-century tenure at M-G-M, Pasternak had specialized in Kathryn Grayson musicals, Mario Lanza musicals, Doris Day musicals and Esther Williams aquatics. The vogue for his kind of picture was in decline, but when M-G-M finally dropped his contract he was able to catch on with Fox. *The Sweet Ride* was a sexy surfing picture, a "programmer" that the Studio hoped to drop into the summer release market for a quick return from the vacationing teenagers who make up the bulk of the drive-in theater audiences. It was not costing much and, if it lost money, it at least supplied the Studio's distribution arm with a product for summer release. In short, *The Sweet Ride* had all the elements of a classic Pasternak film—Technicolor, music (though jazz and rock-and-roll instead of the pop operatics of a traditional Pasternak), youth (the film drew liberally on the Studio's New Talent Program, and its two young co-stars, Michael Sarrazin and Jacqueline Bisset, had been in only a handful of previous pictures), unambiguous story line (aging beach bum Tony Franciosa has protégé beach bum in Sarrazin, protégé beach bum falls in love with sexually mixed-up starlet Bisset, sexually mixed-up starlet is beaten up by her producer after being raped by Hell's Angel-type motorcyclist, Hell's Angel-type motorcyclist is in turn beaten up by the two beach bums, at fadeout protégé beach bum gives up surfing after last perfect wave and goes to work in family's hardware store, vowing to go back to sexually mixed-up starlet when he is worthy of her), and hard-hitting dialogue ("That girl has six broken ribs and a set of bruises that look like a relief map of Tibet").

The week after *The Sweet Ride* began shooting at the beach north of Trancas, Pasternak boarded a chauffeur-driven Studio car for a ride out to the location. He nestled into a corner of the back seat and opened a script he was considering called *Guitar City*. He is a short man on whom the years are beginning to tell. He has closely cropped gray hair, his step is sometimes not quite steady, and he still speaks with a heavy Hungarian accent. The car headed onto the Santa Monica Freeway and then at the beach sped north along the Pacific Coast Highway. Pasternak closed the script and stared out the window.

"You know what the real story for today's kids is?" he said. "It's about an eighteen-year-old girl who fucks but who's afraid to fall in love." He seemed to concentrate on the story possibilities for a while. "The big problem in Hollywood today is replacement. All the big stars are on crutches. You get a young girl falling in love with Cary Grant. In real life, she sleeps with him once or twice to see what it's like, then she leaves him. In Hollywood they live happily ever after."

It was a gray, muggy day and off to the left of the highway, surfers were waiting out beyond the summer combers. The beach and the sand and the water put Pasternak in mind of Esther Williams and he began to ruminate about the pictures he had built around her. "I used to keep her in the water 99 per cent of the time," he said. His lips curled in a tentative smile. "Wet she was a star."

The *Sweet Ride* location was on Point Dume, three miles past Trancas. The Studio had built a road from the highway down to the beach-house set it had rented for two months. The road was necessary to accommodate all the trucks which hauled out equipment from the Studio every day. (Under union rules, nothing could be left on the location overnight. Even the cast could not drive out to the location in the morning; they had to report to the Studio and be driven out in Studio cars.) The script had called for two houses on the beach, but when such a site could not be found, the Studio rented a large house trailer and installed it next to the most suitable house available. The lot behind the house was filled with equipment trucks, portable-dressing-room trucks and portable-bathroom trucks. Cables covered the ground. The crew sat around in chairs reading the trade papers. Pasternak studied the slate-gray sky. "Most days you want sun," he said. "But if you get weather like this, you hope it stays this way all day. The sun comes out now, it's a bad match. And a bad match costs money."

Pasternak picked his way through the cables and between the lights down to a sundeck where *The Sweet Ride*'s director, Harvey Hart, was setting up a shot. "You're running late," Pasternak said.

Hart did not look around. He was sitting in a director's chair decorated with red hearts. He waited until the lights and camera were in the proper position and then gestured wearily up toward the house, where Tony Franciosa was standing, smoking a cigarette.

"Tony showed up an hour late this morning," Hart said. He still had not turned around. "He said he was sick. What can you do? It gets the day off to a bad start."

Pasternak put his hands in his pockets and gazed out

at the ocean. "You know Tony Franciosa doesn't draw flies at the box office," he said.

Hart did not move.

"But he's a good actor," Pasternak said, almost to himself. "You're not buying box office any more. You're buying talent."

He turned around and stared up the steps toward the house. Jacqueline Bisset was standing at the top of the stairs. She is a young English girl in her early twenties. She saw Pasternak looking at her and slowly came down the stairs.

"Good morning, Mr. Pasternak," she said.

"It's afternoon," Pasternak said. The day was going too slowly for him. He looked at her and then smiled. "This girl I love," he said.

Jacqueline Bisset smiled hesitantly.

"That bikini you were wearing yesterday," Pasternak said. "Was it yours?"

"Yes, was something wrong?"

"It looked baggy in the rushes."

"It's not really. It fits."

"Doesn't fit tight enough," Pasternak said. "Get one from wardrobe."

"It fits when it's dry," Jacqueline Bisset said. "It's just that I got such a pounding when I was in the water. It's a terribly long scene." She laughed. The scene called for a wave to wash the top off her bikini. "I had my arms over here"—she crossed her arms over her bosom—"and I couldn't pull the bottom up. Maybe I shouldn't have been so modest. But that's why it didn't look tight. Honest."

"Okay," Pasternak said. He looked at her for a long

time without saying anything. She began to fidget under his gaze, pretending not to notice.

"You got youth on your side," Pasternak said finally. "Doris Day, she thinks she doesn't get old. She tells me once it was her cameraman who was getting older. She wanted me to fire him." The memory seemed to satisfy him. "Ha," he said.

Well, she's fashionably lean,
And she's fashionably late,
She'll never rank a scene,
She'll never break a date;
But she's no drag, just watch the way she walks,
She's a Twentieth Century Fox, she's a Twentieth Century Fox.
No tears, no fears, no ruined years,
No clocks; She's a Twentieth Century Fox.
She's the queen of cool,
And she's the lady who waits,
Since her mind left school,
It never hesitates;
She won't waste time on elementary talk,
She's a Twentieth Century Fox,
She's a Twentieth Century Fox;
Got the world locked up inside a plastic box;
She's a Twentieth Century Fox.

Richard Zanuck was late. The dailies were about to begin and he still had not arrived at his private projection room in the basement of the Studio's administration building. Zanuck watches the dailies—the unedited film shot the previous day on all the Studio's feature pictures—immediately after lunch every day, always in the company of the same executive quintet —Harry Sokolov, his executive assistant, a doughnut-shaped little lawyer and former talent agency vice president; Stan Hough, head of the production department, a rangy, rawboned man with a deceptively open, country face whose father had the same job at the Studio under Darryl Zanuck; Owen McLean, head of the casting department; James Fisher, West Coast story editor; and Barbara McLean, a small bird-like woman who is head of the Studio's cutting department.

It was nearly two o'clock when Zanuck walked into the screening room. He had played two sets of tennis during lunch and he was tieless and carrying his coat over his arm. A trickle of shower water ran down the side of his face. He hung his suit coat neatly on a hanger and began knotting his tie. Flopping into an overstuffed leather chair, he pressed the buzzer notifying the projectionist to begin. The room went dark.

"What have we got, Bobby?" Zanuck asked Barbara McLean.

"We start with the *Joanna* test, Dick," Barbara McLean said. *Joanna* was a picture that the Studio was preparing to shoot in England later in the summer, a contemporary comedy about a provincial girl entangled in the mod morality of London. The picture was being filmed under the Eady Plan, a program by which the British government helps finance a foreign film provided that it is made in the United Kingdom with a predominantly English cast and crew. The enormous success of *Darling, Alfie, Morgan* and *Georgie Girl* had not been lost on the Studio. All had been made with stars then virtually unknown in the U.S., and, instead of trying for mass appeal, all had appealed primarily to the under-thirty audience. The promise of high return for low investment was irresistible, especially with the Eady Plan covering part of the action, and the Studio had seven low-budget contemporary English pictures in preparation. Like the others, *Joanna* would be filmed with comparative unknowns both in front of and behind the cameras.

The film on the projection room screen was of a girl testing for the title role. The girl was tall and angular and she smiled and pulled on a lock of her hair for the camera, shifting back and forth from one foot to the other. Off camera, the director began asking her questions: What was her father like? "Clark Gable." Did she like Clark Gable? "Oh, no, I like my father," the girl said. She brushed the hair back from her face and wet her pouty lips. "He was the best poker player in the Royal Navy. That's what he and my mother got married on." Was her father a gambler? "No," the girl said, "he's a vegetarian."

Zanuck stirred in his seat. A scowl slowly began to rend his brow. He turned to Owen McLean. "I don't care if her father's a vegetarian or not," he said. "Isn't she going to play a scene? What have we got this for?"

"I don't know, Rich," McLean said in the darkness. "I thought she was going to do something from the picture."

"She's in every scene," Zanuck said. "I'd like to see what she looks like doing a scene." His head swiveled around and there were murmurs of agreement.

"Jesus, this is ridiculous," Stan Hough said. "There's a lot of money at stake."

The girl on screen kept wetting her lips. She did a Charlie Chaplin imitation, then sinuously made love to a poster of Clark Gable, her lips synchronized to a Judy Garland record of "You Made Me Love You" playing in the background. Zanuck was getting visibly irritated.

"Don't they have a script over there, Owen?" he said.

"Sure they do, Rich," McLean said.

"Ridiculous," Stan Hough said again. "This girl's in all but ten minutes of the picture."

"They got a script and she's doing Chaplin," Zanuck said.

"And singing Judy Garland records," Hough said.

"It's a goddamn subterfuge," Zanuck said.

"Ridiculous," Hough said.

"I hate this crap," McLean said. He knotted his fingers under his chin. "It's a subterfuge. The girl's the whole picture. Why doesn't he give her a scene to play?" He peered through the darkness. "You know why?"

"I know why," Hough said.

"Jesus, it's clear to me," Zanuck said.

"She's got to be the director's girl friend," McLean said. "She's got to be."

"Got to be," Hough said.

"He would have given her a scene otherwise," Sokolov said.

"Ridiculous," Hough said.

Zanuck flicked on the light by his chair and finished knotting his tie. He got up and took his coat off the hanger. "Goddamn waste of time," he said.

The Sweet Ride was still shooting at the beach. One morning shortly after he arrived on the location Joe Pasternak was accosted by Bob Denver, a loose-jointed young actor who was playing a hippie jazz musician in the picture. Denver was not a piano player and his numbers in the film had been pre-recorded by someone else. Dissatisfied with the pre-recorded piano track, the actor had brought a pianist friend down to the beach and recommended to Pasternak that his friend re-record the piano numbers.

"We've already recorded," Pasternak said. He eyed Denver warily.

"But it's rinky-dink music," Denver said. "It's not in character." His friend hung in the background. Pasternak turned and looked at the pianist, then back at Denver, jerking his thumb over his shoulder.

"Is this guy in the musicians' union?" Pasternak asked.

"No," Denver said.

A triumphant smile creased Pasternak's face. "Then he can't do it."

"This guy's good," Denver said plaintively.

"The guy I got was good," Pasternak said.

"He's got the wrong sound, Mr. Pasternak," Denver said.

Pasternak plucked at the collar of his blue checked shirt. He patted Denver on the arm. "You're a good boy, I'll see," he said. Pasternak watched Denver and the musician stroll off. "Never say no to an actor," he said.

Back at the Studio, *Star!* was in the final stages of its book, or non-musical, shooting. At the conclusion of the book shooting, the company was going to close down for two weeks to rehearse the big musical numbers. An additional two or three weeks had been allotted to shoot the musical numbers. The frame of *Star!* was a time-worn Hollywood storytelling device: Gertrude Lawrence (as played by Julie Andrews) sits in a projection room watching a black-and-white small-screen documentary of her life which periodically dissolves into widescreen, color and stereophonic sequences of what *really* happened. The projection room sequences were all that remained to be shot before the shutdown and Robert Wise had set his cameras up in one of the Studio's actual screening rooms, Projection Room 3-A.

"You know, I really didn't want to make the Gertrude Lawrence story," Wise said as he waited for the shot to be set up. "What I really wanted after *The Sound of Music* was a star vehicle for Julie. It's a touchy business with stars. They want to see scripts before they commit themselves." He cleaned his glasses with a handkerchief. "But I didn't want to hire a writer, buy all the properties about Gertie's life, and then have Julie turn it down. Leaving me stuck with the Gertie Lawrence story. So I had my associates do a tremendous amount of research into Gertie's life, interviewing people, getting anecdotes we could use, an insight into her the books didn't have." He stepped aside as a brace of arc lights were wrestled into position, waiting until they were properly placed before he continued. "Then we explained our concept to Julie. She said she'd do it and that was all we needed to get a script together." He smiled. "Of course, we had to buy all the books then to cover ourselves against a lawsuit."

The shot was finally set up and Julie Andrews was

called from her dressing room. She was wearing a long, tailored purple coat with a velvet collar, matching skirt and shocking-pink blouse, as well as two diamond bracelets, a diamond pin and a double strand of pearls, part of the jewelry on loan from Cartier's and worth approximately $100,000. As she arranged herself in a seat in the front row of the projection room, she picked at the full sleeve of her blouse. "My God, how did they ever wear anything like this?" she said.

"They did, Julie, they did," Wise said soothingly.

The shot was a closeup of Julie Andrews.

NARRATOR:
. . . One can imagine the poignancy of this reunion.

As the narrator is speaking, we hear a sudden loud, joyous peal of feminine laughter. The adult GERTIE *(in color), who has been watching the small-screen documentary, gets up into frame, moves toward the screen, the back of her head in the projector's throw, hiding the black and white picture. We are in:*

21 INTERIOR—PROJECTION THEATER—NEW YORK—1940 —DAY

As Gertie appears, the screen opens out and we are in "our" picture—in widescreen color. The black and white picture of the small screen stops, holding the frame of the Music Hall as Gertie turns to face camera, still laughing.

Wise stood by the camera reading Julie Andrews' cue line—"One can imagine the poignancy of this reunion." After each take, Wise asked for one more: a strand of hair on Julie Andrews' wig had fallen out of place; the projector flickering in the back of the shot was not lit. "Fine, good," Wise said. "I like it. Let's have one more."

Julie Andrews experimented with gestures and business. "It started off funny, but I thought it picked up in the middle," she said after one take. "But my eyes were so damn busy."

"That's okay," Wise said. "We picked up that business with the eyes. I like it. Let's use it again in the next take."

The shot was finally completed and the stand-ins moved to their places so that the lights and camera could be positioned for the next setup. Julie Andrews flopped into a chair in her dressing room outside Projection Room 3-A. A makeup woman wiped her face with a piece of Kleenex. The unit publicist knocked on the dressing room door and asked if she were free for an interview with a visiting journalist from Chicago.

"Just a minute, luv," she said. "Those damn lights. I've got to catch my breath."

"It will only be a short one, Julie," the publicist said.

"Only till they set up the next shot," Julie Andrews said. She pressed her hands against her eyebrows. "These damn interviews."

"This one will be twenty minutes at most, Julie," the publicist said.

"Well, if it will help get back ten million dollars," Julie Andrews said, "what's twenty minutes?"

Richard Zanuck settled into his chair to watch the dailies, and the lights in the screening room dimmed.

"What do we have?" he asked Barbara McLean.

"*Star!*, a *Tony Rome* trailer, and Walter Doniger wants you to take a look at a scene from *Peyton Place*." Doniger was one of the three rotating directors of the television serial. It was rare that Zanuck watched any television rushes. "It was a tough one and he thinks it came off pretty well."

Zanuck grunted. The *Star!* footage flickered on the screen. It was the projection room sequence shot from a variety of different angles. No one in the small room spoke. The phone rang and Zanuck picked it up. It was his broker.

"What's it up to?" he said softly into the telephone. He listened while the *Star!* footage ended and the trailer (or coming attractions preview) for *Tony Rome,* a detective thriller starring Frank Sinatra, came on screen. "Shall we dump it at the opening?" Zanuck said to his caller. He listened again. "Okay, let's hold it for a couple of days and then we'll see."

He clicked off the phone and turned his attention back to the screen. The *Tony Rome* trailer had a narrator's voice-over, and the sound of it made Zanuck fidget in his chair.

"I hate that guy's voice," he said. "It's terrible. Change it." He turned on a table light and glanced at his watch. "I've got an appointment at three o'clock. What's left?"

"The *Peyton Place* stuff Doniger wanted you to see," Barbara McLean said.

Zanuck hesitated for a moment. "Tell Walter I saw it and thought it was great," he said. He picked up his coat and headed for the door.

Stan Hough laughed. "Maybe what he wanted you to see was a mile-long negative scratch."

"Jesus," Zanuck said. "You don't think." He smiled and disappeared through the door.

Zanuck's appointment was with Paul Monash, executive producer of both *Peyton Place* and *Judd,* another television series. A handsome, nervous man of fifty, Monash was also producing his first feature picture for the Studio, a thriller called *Deadfall,* starring Michael Caine. The film was being made in Europe and Monash actually did not have much to do with it. All he could really do was watch the dailies when they were shipped in and, when something caught his eye, talk occasionally to the film's director, Bryan Forbes, on the telephone. It was not a very satisfactory arrangement but, for Monash, *Deadfall* was at least an entree into feature film production. At the moment, he was concerned with Giovanna Ralli, an Italian actress who was Caine's co-star and love interest in *Deadfall* and who was having a great deal of trouble with her English. Much of her dialogue would have to be "looped," or dubbed, in post-production.

"She's intelligible for the most part, but she just can't think in English," Monash said. His lips seemed set in a self-deprecating half smile. "So it's really slow. I talked to Bryan on the phone and he's having a terrible time. She doesn't come off badly. I mean, she's got a lot of presence, but it just takes so many takes."

"Can we dub her?" Zanuck said.

"Not without her permission," Monash said. "That's her deal."

"What's Bryan say?" Zanuck said.

"He thinks he's got an out," Monash said. "He says he's going to tell her she's got 500 loops and when she hears that, maybe she'll get discouraged and let someone else dub."

Zanuck methodically folded a piece of paper and slit

it open with a letter opener. "She's not going to be that easy to dub," he said finally. "I've been watching her in the dailies. Her mouth just kind of fumbles around. It'll be tough, real tough."

The following week, Monash called and asked if I wanted to drive out to the Desilu lot in Culver City, where the Studio rented space for the filming of his TV series, *Judd*. Monash divided each day between the Fox lot in Westwood, where he spent mornings working on *Peyton Place* and *Deadfall*, and Desilu, where he went after lunch every afternoon to oversee *Judd*, a melodrama whose hero was a peripatetic lawyer in the F. Lee Bailey mold. *Judd* was a new show, scheduled to begin on the ABC Television Network that fall, and Monash was hopeful that, within the limits of television's taboos, it could dip into social criticism in much the same manner as had *The Defenders*, another earnest liberal series about the legal profession.

"I'll make $500,000 this year," Monash said from behind the wheel of his blue Corvette Sting Ray on the way over to Culver City. "Maybe five-fifty. And I've got all the deals going for me. I only take $2,500 a week and spread the rest of it out. And now I'm going into depreciation. There's a multi-million-dollar apartment project I'm involved in down in Fort Worth. You can spread the depreciation out to avoid the tax bite. If the project burns down, what the hell? So much the better."

The Sting Ray halted at a stoplight. Monash let the motor idle. A car pulled up alongside. When the light turned, Monash gunned his motor, leaving the other car in his wake.

"I've got a house in Mandeville Canyon, I walk in the

peace marches and I worry about Watts," Monash said. "How can I improve things?" He laughed dryly at himself. "It's academic to worry about the rats in Watts when you're making half a million a year. You think you're being realistic, but how many Negroes are going to move into Mandeville Canyon?"

It was a ten-minute ride to Desilu. Monash parked his car in his space and walked into his bungalow. His office was austere to the point of anonymity. There was a typewriter at his desk along with a Roget's Thesaurus and the American College Dictionary. In the bookcase was a twenty-volume set entitled *Speeches and Papers of the Presidents*. There was also a small kitchen stocked with diet soft drinks. The sink was littered with dirty dishes.

Monash opened a Fresca and collapsed into a chair. "You know, I'm in therapy," he said. "It's an old story, but it's given me an insight into myself. I'm a big producer, but what do I do? I'm not doing anything on *Deadfall* and the TV shows take care of themselves. Bryan Forbes says he's directing *Deadfall* for the money, to give him the loot to do a good picture. So much for *Deadfall*." His eyes and lips crinkled wistfully. "Maybe I should write a book. I'd like to take a year off and do a book on the Detroit riots." He pulled on the soda bottle. "Of course, there wouldn't be any motion picture rights for something like a book on the riots. But it would give me the feeling of accomplishing something. Maybe I will." He shifted his position in the chair. "A friend of mine got $175,000 paperback for a book he wrote."

Monash kicked off his alligator loafers and began

rubbing his feet. "Hollywood gets to you after a while," he said. "My wife went to Europe to visit her family and so I went to the bank and got her some traveler's checks to cover her expenses. She comes back and I asked her if she spent it. 'Not all of it,' she says. I ask for it back. 'No,' she says, 'it's mine.' I say it's ours. Well, it's been a running situation ever since she got back. This morning she takes the checks and showers them on me." He seemed to consider the scene and its possible effect on me. "It's a real Hollywood story," he added.

Monash took the bottle of soda and deposited it in the kitchen on top of the dirty dishes. He came back and sprawled into the chair again.

"Are you happy?" he said suddenly.

5

" I'm Tomo from Andro, "

Irwin Allen said

By the end of the summer, the Studio's television department had eight series in preparation for the upcoming season: two new ones, *Judd* and *Custer*, the latter a deodorized Western about the life and times of General George Armstrong Custer: and six holdovers from previous seasons, *Peyton Place*, *Batman*, *Felony Squad*, *Daniel Boone*, *Voyage to the Bottom of the Sea* and *Lost in Space*. Even then, however, the television department was making plans for the season a year hence, calculating how many shows might be canceled during the forthcoming season, estimating what formats the networks might favor a year or even two years in the future (was the campy *Batman* cycle played out, were

Westerns or detective series coming back into vogue, what kind of hero needed a Negro sidekick?). Scripts were read, prospects weighed. The stakes were high. The cost of making a pilot film for television had become so prohibitive—sometimes in excess of $500,000 —and the chances of selling that pilot to one of the three networks so slim—roughly one chance in ten— that a few errors in judgment could cost a studio several million dollars and the executive who made the errors his job. Many studios tried to cut their losses by showing the networks a "spinoff" episode from an existing show, using the new characters and plot situation within the framework and budget of a show already on the air, or simply, if their past track record was good, going to the networks with only a package and a pilot script and presentation.

Either possibility posed enormous problems for Irwin Allen, who created and produced two science-fiction series for the Studio, *Voyage to the Bottom of the Sea* and *Lost in Space*. Allen's sci-fis were so enormously complicated and utilized so many special effects that it was difficult to visualize a concept for a new series from a script. Rather than shoot an enormously expensive pilot, he had settled on the solution of showing the network a ten-minute presentation film that sketched out the main situation and visual highlights of the proposed series. The presentation films had no plot and were only ten minutes long, but each one cost in the vicinity of $100,000.

One afternoon late in the summer, Allen assembled his production staff in his office to discuss a new science-fiction project that he was presenting to CBS called *The Man from the 25th Century*. The color scheme in Allen's office on the second floor of the Old Administration Building is based on a rather lurid orange. The couches and chairs are orange leather, and by the window, casting its baleful red globular eyes over the office, is a large robot, a prop from *Lost in Space*. On one wall are graphs, sketches, charts and paintings of new sci-fis that Allen has in preparation—*Aladdin, Safari, City Beneath the Sea* and *The Man from the 25th Century*. A bookcase was filled with promotional material for each segment of the two shows Allen then had on the air, *Lost in Space* and *Voyage to the Bottom of the Sea*—toy robots, miniature submarines, rubber fright masks (for a segment of *Voyage* titled "Man of Many Faces," Allen had sent every major television editor in the country a rubber mask used by the Man of Many Faces). On the floor below, Allen had a full-time crew of artists sketching storyboards for each segment of his shows, as well as a staff of researchers compiling all available information on time, space, the ocean and giants, for possible use as both effects and plot points on his current and proposed series. In the presentation script of *City Beneath the Sea*, there was an eight-page appendix of "new underseas projects and discoveries to be used in combination or alone as premises for *City Beneath the Sea* episodes." Among the projects and discoveries were:

Bubble curtains for use as fish pens;
Acoustical barriers, electrical fields and temperature fences for the same purpose;
New methods for tagging fish using radioactive markers to help discover secrets of migration;
Extracting oxygen from water by use of a silicone membrane.

In all, the researchers had compiled sixty possible discoveries. "I've tried to take the lunacy that exists in television and reduce it to a quiet panic," Allen told me one day. "There's only one thing to remember about television: it's a business."

He is a large, myopic, hirsute man with hair like Brillo and a bowl-shaped paunch that leaks out between the bottom of his shirt and the top of his trousers. He has a raucous voice and he is richly sarcastic, but it is largely a performance without a cutting edge. He supervises even the most minute details of his shows. There were a half dozen people present at *The Man from the 25th Century* meeting and each had a copy of the presentation script Allen had written:

THE MAN FROM THE 25TH CENTURY is a one-hour weekly television series of science-fiction, high adventure and action. It is the eerily horrifying tale of Andro, our nearest planetary neighbor, whose source of power is being used far more quickly than it can be created and whose need to attack the Earth and replenish such power is of the highest priority. An Earthling, kidnapped in infancy and transported to Andro for indoctrination, is returned to Earth to start its downfall. He is repelled by his assignment and defects to the Earthlings. Each week the non-humans from Andro arrive in flying saucers and create havoc with Earth. Each week the Earthlings, aided by THE MAN FROM THE 25TH CENTURY and his weaponry, succeed in dissuading the enemy.

On succeeding pages, Allen's script spelled out the show's theme ("The basic theme dramatizes man's earliest hidden fear—the appearance of seemingly extraterrestrial beings from another planet"), its major settings ("The planet Andro, two-and-a-half light-years from Earth, the super metropolis of the future in the year 2467" and "Project Delphi, most mysterious of all undertakings in the history of the United States government," buried underground deep beneath Glacier National Park and dedicated to combating the attack from Andro), and its leading character, Tomo, The Man from the 25th Century ("Tomo—twenty-four years old—the kidnapped Earthling. Dark, handsome, six feet, three inches tall. He is the most unusual of men. Graduate of the sciences of Nali, the great technological studies offered by the scientists of the planet Andro. Brilliant, trained to kill, and a master in the art of self-defense. Hidden deep within is a warm friendly nature. But so penetrating was his indoctrination, even he is unaware of his second personality").

The problem before the meeting was whether to spin *The Man from the 25th Century* off a segment of *Lost in Space* or to go with a ten-minute presentation film. The discussion was scarcely underway when there was a knock on the door and the unit production manager for *Voyage to the Bottom of the Sea* entered the office, muttering apologies. A *Voyage* episode scheduled to start shooting the following week had a character called Lobster Man, and the wardrobe department had been unable to make his costume as specified in the designer's sketches.

"Irwin, the antennae on Lobster Man's suit are supposed to vibrate, but the suit isn't rigged for it," the production manager said.

Allen threw up his hands in resignation. "Is it a big story point?"

"No," the unit man said.

"Then forget it." Allen thought for a moment, rubbing his hands over his paunch. "Wait a minute," he said. "Ask the electrical department if they can put two little blinking lights in the antennae."

"Okay," the production man said. "That's a good idea, Irwin."

"That's what I'm sitting in the boss's chair for," Allen said. "You got a little problem about Lobster Man, you come to see Irwin."

Allen turned back to *The Man from the 25th Century*. On an easel at the end of the table were color sketches of Andro and of the "interrogation room" at Delphi. The art director, a young man named Dale Hennesy, lifted the overlays from the sketches and displayed them for Allen.

"If we spin off from *Space*, we're going to have to get a script written quick, Irwin," said Hal Herman, one of Allen's production managers.

"No problem," Allen said. "Irwin knows how to do it. The Space Family Robinson"—the family in *Lost in Space*—"turns up on another planet. They settle down for dinner and then all of a sudden this beautiful man appears. They reach for their ray guns and this guy says, 'I'm Tomo from Andro,' and to pay for his supper, he tells a story. Dissolve—*The Man from the 25th Century*." He patted the presentation script. "It's all here. Easy, right?"

"Right, Irwin," chorused the table.

Allen doodled for a moment with a pencil. "Say we do spin off," he said. "We spin off where?"

"The twenty-second segment," Hal Herman said.

"That starts shooting twenty-five working days from

now," Allen said, checking his production schedule. He turned to Dale Hennesy. "Dale, using spit and glue—and with a start date that close, that's what you're going to have to use—can you get these sets together by then?"

Hennesy whistled softly. "Can do," he said finally.

Allen asked to see the rest of the sketches. One drawing showed the concrete living quarters at Project Delhi. Allen shook his head. "It doesn't send me," he said.

"What I was trying to do here, Irwin . . ." Hennesy began.

Allen shook his head vigorously. "Dale, it doesn't send me," he said in measured tones. "Let's just accept that. It wastes time to argue and time is what?"

"Money, Irwin," Hennesy said.

"Right," Allen said.

He perused the rest of the sketches. Gradually he began to abandon the idea of spinning *The Man from the 25th Century* off a *Lost in Space* segment. While the production problems of a spinoff were not insurmountable, they would pose certain difficulties and furthermore would strain the already tight budget of the show. As the meeting wore on, Allen began to think in terms of the ten-minute presentation film. He asked Hennesy for the storyboard sketches of the originally proposed spinoff segment.

"I don't like these much, Dale," Allen said. He was beating time on the conference table with his knuckles. "They're okay for a storyboard, but not for a presentation film. We need something flashier."

Hennesy nodded.

"And I think it's a mistake to show story continuity

in a presentation film," Allen said. "We're not trying to sell a story, we're trying to sell a concept."

"How about using paintings?" Hennesy said. "I mean, the paintings of the various sets?"

Allen slapped his hand on the desk. "Great," he said. "We can use the camera to get a sense of movement. Move in, pan, hold, dissolve through. Great. The paintings are static, but the camera moves." He turned to Hal Herman. "How long will it take five artists to do thirty paintings from our sketches?"

Herman figured on a pad. "Twelve working days," he said finally.

"Figure fifteen," Allen said. "Now I'm a sucker for blue, so if you want to win me over, use a lot of blue. Allen Blue, I call it." He got up from his chair and wiped his glasses on his shirt. A secretary brought him a glass of orange juice and told him that the unit man from *Voyage to the Bottom of the Sea* had returned and wanted to see him.

"Now what's the matter?" Allen said when the unit man came into the office.

"About Lobster Man, Irwin," the unit man said. "The lights in the antennae won't work."

"I don't believe won't work," Allen said.

"There's too much voltage, Irwin."

"Then Lobster Man will fry?" Allen said.

"Right, Irwin."

Allen patted the unit man on the shoulder. "Paul," he said, "*you* figure something out. You be Irwin for a while. I trust you implicitly, Paul." He dismissed the unit man with a wave of his hand and turned back to the conference table. "Okay, we're agreed," he said. "The presentation film, right?"

"Right, Irwin."

"We've got $100,000 to work with," Allen said. "Not a penny more. *Not a penny*. Right? Right."

The next day was Wednesday, and, as on every Wednesday, there was a conference in Jack Baur's office of all the Studio's casting directors for both features and television. A handsome, sedate man who looks like a bank vice president, Baur is the assistant head of the casting department. His daughter, Elizabeth, was one of the young actresses in the Studio's New Talent Program. Present at the meeting were Bill Kinney, casting director for *Judd* and *Felony Squad,* Joe Scully for *Peyton Place* and *Valley of the Dolls,* Larry Stewart for the Irwin Allen shows, Ross Brown for *Daniel Boone* and *Custer,* Carl Joy for stunt men and extra talent, and Curt Conway and Pamela Danova of the New Talent School.

"I need two 7⅜ heads," Larry Stewart said.

"Two what?" Baur said.

"Two 7⅜ heads," Stewart said. "To play monsters on *Lost in Space*. The art department has already whipped up the heads and they happen to be 7⅜. Now we just need the actors to fit them."

Baur shook his head. "All right, everyone keep a lookout for 7⅜ heads," he said. He shuffled through the papers piled in front of him. "Okay, we've got a lot of commitments on play-or-pay deals, so let's see if we can place them." He picked up one of the papers. "Charlie Robinson," he said. "He's got a $10,000 guarantee and we're converting it to a term contract at $500 a week. Any pictures or TV shows we can use him on? It's play-or-pay, remember."

"No go on *Felony Squad*," Bill Kinney said. He drew a square in the air with his fingers.

"How about *Peyton Place?*" Baur asked.

Joe Scully shook his head and he too doodled a square in the air.

There was laughter around the table. "Your enthusiasm overwhelms me," Baur said. "Well, he should be a cinch for *Tora, Tora, Tora*. He can always play a young Naval officer."

"And he's square enough to use in *Tom Swift*," Kinney said.

"Okay," Baur said. "Fun is fun, but don't forget, this is a $10,000 knock." He began to check up on the week's activities with each of the casting directors. "How about *Judd*, Bill?" he asked Kinney.

"We sent a script to Ian Bannen and he likes it," Kinney said. "But he has to check with his accountant in London to see if he has enough days left in this country to beat the tax rap."

"How much they offer him?" Baur said.

"$3,500," Kinney said. "It's the same thing with all these English guys. He doesn't want to cut into his few days left here if he can still get a picture in this country. You know, the money."

Baur checked his notes again. "As you know, we've got a new series on the back burner called *European Eye*. It's about a private eye based in London who takes on any American in Europe who gets in trouble. It should be exciting. Locations all over Europe. We need a name leading man. Cliff Robertson, Hugh O'Brian, Mickey Callan—you know, one of those half-baked guys who want to do pictures."

"And can't get any," Kinney said.

Baur shrugged. *"Daniel Boone?"* he said. "What do you need, Ross?"

"Are there any young fops in the New Talent Program?" Ross Brown said. "I need a young fop for *Boone.*"

"What's the role?" Baur said.

"Just that," Brown said. "A young fop. The story's about this Indian girl and she's living with these white folks. They find out she's an Indian and they don't want her to marry their young fop son."

"Richard Krisher," Curt Conway said. "A perfect fop. A Billy DeWolfe type, only younger."

Brown looked at his clipboard. He mentioned another young actor in the New Talent Program. "Has he been drafted yet?" he asked. "I need him to play an Indian."

"He's got blue eyes," Baur said.

"Hazel," Brown said. "It can work."

"Hell, yes," Scully said. "They were making a Western over at Universal a couple of years ago, in color, and when they looked at the dailies, they discovered that the Indian chief had blue eyes. It was too late to replace him, so they put the research department to work and they found a tribe in North Dakota or someplace where every redskin had blue eyes. They wrote in a line of dialogue to cover it and they were home free."

Elizabeth Bergner is houseguesting with Mildred Natwick here. Catching up with her at her lawyer Arnold Weissberger's Sutton Place apartment, I was reminded of what George Bernard Shaw said about her in my

*memorable visit with him the summer before he died:
"Miss Bergner played Joan as if she were being burned
at the stake when the curtain went up, instead of when
it went down." In spite of this wicked appraisal, Elizabeth
has clung through the years to the letters G.B.S. has
written her, but now she has turned them—and her cor-
respondence with James M. Barrie, who wrote his final
play,* The Boy David, *for her—over to Sotheby's for auc-
tion. They should net her a tidy sum, which, I assume, is
the reason she's selling them.*

Radie Harris, The Hollywood Reporter

The background music of *Dr. Dolittle,* meanwhile,
was still being arranged and scored. The task of arrang-
ing Leslie Bricusse's original score into background ac-
companiment fell to Lionel Newman, head of the Studio's music department, and his associate, Alexander
Courage. Film scoring is an enormously tedious job. Because it must be timed exactly to the action on the
screen, it is recorded in snippets sometimes only a few
seconds long. The scoring of *Dr. Dolittle* presented another problem not usually encountered in film musicals. The normal procedure is for the cast to pre-record
musical production numbers before a full studio orchestra; then, when the number is actually filmed, the
actors mouth their lyrics to a recorded playback. Rex
Harrison, however, refused to do a playback; he argued
that he was an actor, not a singer, and that it was difficult for him to act convincingly while trying to follow a
playback. He insisted on being recorded live while his
numbers were being shot, accompanied only by a piano
on the set. The full orchestral background was mixed in
later. The process was costly and time-consuming, but
it was the only one to which Harrison would agree.

"He's the star, so what are you going to do?" Newman said one morning as he and Courage worked on the arrangement of the music behind the main titles of *Dr. Dolittle*. He is a stocky, gray-haired man whose conversation is sprinkled with pleasant obscenities. On the table in front of him was a plate of doughnuts and a cue sheet of the proposed title music. The sheet was marked into segments timed down to one-third of a second.

"We've got animated titles," Newman said. "The problem is we got to make it cute without making it Disney goddamn pixie."

Courage held a stopwatch in his hand. "We've got fifty seconds here," he said. "Maybe we can drop 'Talk to the Animals' in this spot."

"Ready when you are," Newman said.

Courage set the stopwatch. "Go," he said.

Newman began to hum "Talk to the Animals," waving his pencil as if it were a baton. "Da, da, da, da, DA, da, da, dee, dee, dee, da, da, da, da, dee."

He finished and looked at Courage. "Fifty-seven seconds," Courage said."

"Shit," Newman said. "It's such a lousy song anyway. So what do we use?"

Courage mentioned another song from the score. "That's not so hot, either," Newman said. "But at least it's got melody."

He hummed the new song, banging his pencil on the table, while Courage clocked him. "Great," Courage said, when Newman finished. "With five seconds schlemming around, I think we got it." He checked the cue sheet. "That will take us up to the associate producer's credit."

"Great," Newman said. "We got time up the ass."

A few days later, Newman was on Sound Stage 1, where he was conducting the Studio orchestra while they recorded a portion of the background score. The blower was out of order and the stage was hot and reeked of sweat. Instrument cases were scattered around the floor. There were fifty-eight players in the orchestra, all of them dressed in sport shirts and loose-fitting muumuus. That day's call sheet called for the orchestra to record twenty-six pieces of music, ranging from thirty seconds to four minutes long. Newman stood on a podium in front of the orchestra, a set of earphones over his head, facing a screen on which the scenes to be scored were projected. The scenes were in black and white and the dialogue had been erased from the sound track so as not to distract the orchestra. Beside Newman on the podium was an enormous timer.

Newman pulled at his gray polo shirt. "Jesus, isn't there any air in here?" he said. He sniffed the air around him. "I know I don't smell this bad all the time."

He called for a take. The shot was an insert of Dr. Dolittle peering out from a window in the prison on the floating island of Popsipetel where he had been incarcerated. The shot then cut to an exterior view of the native village, which was covered by a thick carpet of frost. A red "Take" sign flashed over the screen. The orchestra began to play, a slow, menacing staccato underscored by the beat of drums. The take lasted thirty-two seconds.

"Jesus, you're great," Newman said. "The Lionel Newman Philharmonic Orchestra."

He gave the orchestra a five-minute break and asked for a playback. The film flashed on the screen again, this time with the dialogue and the music. Newman listened intently. The music drowned out the dialogue, but it would ultimately be mixed with the screen sounds so that everything would be perfectly modulated. Just as the playback ended, Arthur Jacobs walked onto the stage.

"Hello, lardass," Newman said amiably. He turned to the orchestra. "This is Mr. Apjac. He's the tiger in your tank." Jacobs looked disconcerted, his sad, dark eyes nervously flickering back and forth between Newman and the orchestra.

"Listen, lardass," Newman said, "is there any chance we can get a longer shot in the percussion sequence? As it stands now, the percussion comes right in on the dialogue."

"I think we can get you a few extra feet," Jacobs said.

"That's all I want, Arthur," Newman said. "You do that for me, I'll stop telling these people what a lardass you are."

Jacobs took a seat at the rear of the stage, drumming his fingers on a cello case while Newman recorded another piece of music. When the take was over, a dapper little man walked onto the stage. His name was Happy Goday and he was the song plugger Jacobs had hired at $500 a week to get singers to record the *Dolittle* songs.

"Arthur, I got to tell you," Goday said in a raspy little voice. "I got Kate Smith interested."

"That's a thrill," Jacobs said.

"Don't knock it, Arthur," Goday said. "She's very big with the 'God Bless America' crowd."

"So?" Jacobs said.

"Arthur, you're not thinking," Goday said. "You get them and they take their grandkids to the picture, you can stay home and count your money. You're home free, Arthur. Get it?"

Jacobs smiled and began to hum the first bars of "God Bless America."

Jacobs was also producing *Planet of the Apes*, a melodrama about a civilization where apes and men had reversed their roles. The picture starred Charlton Heston as an astronaut whose spaceship had catapulted through the time barrier and crashed on an uncharted planet ruled by an ape society. With the exception of Heston, all the picture's stars—Kim Hunter, Roddy McDowall, James Daly and James Whitmore—played apes. The makeup problems were staggering. Initial substances employed to change human features into the likeness of simians stiffened on the actors' faces so that their features were neither mobile or expressive. Nor could the actors chew, suggesting that they would have to subsist on a liquid diet during the shooting of the film. Experimentation with new rubber compounds resulted in the development of materials that permitted full facial mobility and allowed the actor's skin to breathe inside the heavy layer of ape makeup. But in the first tests, the makeup required six hours to apply and three to remove. Ultimately the Studio makeup department got the application time down to three hours and the removal to one. In actual filming, other problems arose. The dark furry makeup offered nothing other than eyes that could be effectively highlighted. And since the actors wore false protruding jaws fitted with ape-like incisors, care had to be taken in lighting and the selection of camera angles so that both the actors' real and ape teeth were not visible on film.

The afternoon after the *Dr. Dolittle* scoring session, Jacobs drove his golf cart over to Stage 9, where *Planet of the Apes* was filming. As he came on the set with Mort Abrahams, an ape waved and said, "Hello, Mr. Jacobs."

"Hi, hi, how are you?" Jacobs said. He lit a brown cigarette. "Who the hell was that?" he asked Abrahams. "You see someone in ape drag, you don't know who the hell it is."

Jacobs hoisted himself into a director's chair. "Animals on *Dolittle*, apes here," he said to no one in particular. "You think you got problems? Try apes and animals."

"And Rex Harrison," Abrahams said.

Jacobs sighed. "And Rex."

He flicked some ashes off his brown V-necked sweater. "Why do I always pick the tough ones?" he said. He waved a hand in the general direction of a group of apes. "I've been involved with this one for three years," he said. "Three years and $360,000. I took an option on the novel in 1964. Every studio in town turned it down. 'Who needs from apes?' they said. A legitimate question. So I decided I had to have a concept. I hired a lot of art directors and they all did sketches, you know, ape drag and that kind of stuff. Still no sale. Finally Warner's said they'd take a chance and we got Rod Serling to do a script. Then they couldn't budget it. They dropped the whole thing and sold it back to me for all the money they put into it. Three hundred and sixty grand. When I came over to Fox with *Dolittle,* I pre-

sented it to Dick Zanuck." He smiled as he remem-
bered. "A present like that he didn't need. But every
time I came into his office I brought it up. It got so I
never even got the name of the picture out of my
mouth. I'd say, 'Dick, what about . . .' and he'd say,
'No.' You got to hear Dick Zanuck say, 'No.' He means
'No.' But I worked on him and finally I got him to agree
to a test to see how people looked as apes. We wrote a
long dialogue scene, you know, so you could see their
faces moving. Well, Dick liked it and said he wanted to
show it to Darryl. So we brought it to New York." He
ground out the cigarette under his shoe. "Jesus, there
were nine guys in that screening room watching the
test. If any one of them laughed, we were dead. But
they didn't laugh and we were in business."

"And now you got apes and animals, Arthur," Abrahams said.

"And Rex," Jacobs said.

Pandro S. Berman sat in the anteroom outside Richard Zanuck's office. He is a short man, in his sixties,
with monogrammed shirts and a modulated voice seemingly half an octave above where it should be. He had
been a staff producer at M-G-M for years and had come
over to Fox at the same time that Joe Pasternak did. In
his lap was a copy of a script adapted from Lawrence
Durrell's novel, *Justine*, that he had been assigned to
produce under his new contract with the Studio.

"You never change much, Mr. Berman," one of Zanuck's secretaries said.

"Well, thank you, dear, that's a compliment, especially if you've been around as long as I have," Berman
said.

"Oh, you haven't been around that long," the secretary said.

"Oh, yes, I have," Berman said. "I started out at the old FBO Studios when I was eighteen years old. There was a writer at the studio at that time, he couldn't have been more than twenty-three or twenty-four years old, and he was one of the most successful writers in Hollywood. Do you know who that writer was?"

The secretary shook her head.

"Darryl Zanuck," Berman said. His head nodded up and down. "That's how long I've been around. Joseph P. Kennedy owned the studio then. I was making $25 a week and I wanted a raise. We never saw Mr. Kennedy, but I waited by the front door for thirty days and it finally paid off. On the thirtieth day, Mr. Kennedy came out and I asked him for a raise and he raised me five dollars right on the spot, to $30 a week."

"Those must have been wonderful days," the secretary said.

"Oh, they were," Berman said.

"Do you ever remember an actress called Marjorie Reynolds?" the secretary said.

"I certainly do," Berman said.

The secretary pointed to the other typist, a slender redheaded girl with a bouffant hairdo. "That's her daughter."

"Is that a fact?" Berman said. "Marjorie Reynolds the movie star. Well, you're a lot taller than your mother."

"No, we're the same size," Marjorie Reynolds' daughter said. "Maybe it's because my hair is different."

"That must be it," Berman said, "because you certainly look a lot taller than your mother."

Zanuck was finally free and Berman went into his

office. The Studio had poured a great deal of money into *Justine*. It was one of Darryl Zanuck's pet projects. There had been a number of scripts written, the latest by Ivan Moffatt, a former Hollywood writer now living in England. Moffatt had worked on *Justine* with Darryl Zanuck, then had returned to Hollywood to polish the screenplay with Berman.

"I think it's a good screenplay, Richard, a very good screenplay," Berman said. "My wife liked it and she and Ivan got along perfectly. But Larry Marcus is in town and he's just dying to do this picture."

Zanuck did not know Marcus and asked to be briefed.

"Well, Richard, I knew him years ago when he was doing little melodramas, but now he's very big with those new young English directors. He just finished *Petulia* for Richard Lester, that's the new Julie Christie picture, and that's going to be very big, a very big picture, Richard. Metro wants him to do a screenplay—as a matter of fact, he was just over there this morning—but he would postpone that commitment if he thought he could do this picture."

Zanuck pulled at a hangnail. "What's wrong with Ivan's screenplay?" he said without looking up.

"Nothing, nothing at all, Richard," Berman said. "But the thing is, I think we're agreed that we'd like to get one of those bright new English directors on this picture, Lindsay Anderson or John Schlesinger, and I just thought it would be easier if we approached them with a writer they knew and respected."

"Has he read the script?" Zanuck said.

"I gave him a copy and he promised he would read it this very evening," Berman said. "As you know, I sent a copy to Schlesinger and Nelson and I think if we could tell them that we had Larry Marcus, well, I just think we could get a deal."

Zanuck was now gnawing on a knuckle. "Well, let's see what he says after he reads the script."

"This is really putting the cart before the horse," Richard Zanuck said later about *Justine*. "You get a director and naturally he's going to want to make some changes, so then you get another writer. But this way is really putting the cart before the horse. You don't know if Schlesinger or Anderson will even do the picture—or if they'll want Marcus if they do do it."

MARCUS INKED BY 20TH
Larry Marcus has been signed by 20th-Fox to write the final screenplay of the Pandro S. Berman production of Justine, *it was announced today by Richard D. Zanuck, vice president in charge of production.*

The Hollywood Reporter

"The time to hit in this town is before your first picture comes out," the young agent said. He was sitting in a Beverly Hills restaurant sipping an Americano. He ordered a steak rare with French-fried potatoes. "You get the word-of-mouth going. Nobody's seen the picture. It can be a piece of shit, but who knows? You get the word-of-mouth going, you can start making deals all over town. We handle a guy"—he mentioned a young director—"who just finished a picture over at Paramount. Nobody's seen it, but you spread the word that George Cukor loved it. Somebody tells somebody else George Cukor loved it and pretty soon you're not in if you haven't seen it and said it was sensational. Nata-

lie Wood, Arthur Jacobs, they all *loved* it. Who cares
if they've seen it? It's the names that count. Once the
word-of-mouth momentum gets going, you move in.
The guy's locked in for six pictures all over town. If the
picture's good, fine, but if it stinks, he's still set up for a
ton." He asked the waitress for a bottle of Worcester-
shire sauce. "You fail upward here. A guy makes a ten-
million-dollar bomb, the big thing is not that he's
made a bomb, but that he put together a ten-million-
dollar picture. Next time out, they give him a twelve-
million-dollar picture. It's crazy, but that's how it
works. The worst thing that can happen to you is to
have a small success. You make a picture for seven-
fifty, it's a nice picture, it makes a little money, but
you're dead. They aren't interested in pictures that
make a little money. Everybody's looking for the killing.
So you bomb out at ten million. Well, you put together a
big one, and the next time out, you might hit with one."

"The deal, that's all this business is about," a Studio
producer told me a few days later over lunch in the
commissary. "Who's available, when can you get him,
start date, stop date, percentages—the deal, it's the
only thing that matters. Listen, if Paul Newman comes
in and says he wants to play Gertrude Lawrence in
Star!, you do it, that's the nature of the business."

The Sweet Ride was three days behind schedule. Joe
Pasternak watched the morning's shooting at the beach
and when the crew broke found a place beside director
Harvey Hart at the lunch table. Luncheon was served in
a large circus tent set up on a cliff overlooking the surf.

Someone brought him a plate of cold cuts, some fruit juice and a plate of Jello. Pasternak wiped off his fork with a paper napkin.

"We're already three days over," he said to Hart.

"It all evens out, Joe," Hart said. "I heard the Sinatra picture came in fourteen days early."

"Frank must have had a date," Pasternak said.

"DOLITTLE" AIRS TO DEBUT
Monte Carlo—First public introduction of songs from the Arthur P. Jacobs production of Dr. *Dolittle for 20th-Fox will be given by Bobby Darin today when he headlines Princess Grace's annual Red Cross gala here.*
The Hollywood Reporter

The publicity campaign for *Dr. Dolittle* was being handled by the Beverly Hills public relations firm of Rogers, Cowan & Brenner, where Arthur Jacobs had once been a partner before branching into independent film production. Bobby Darin was also a client of Rogers, Cowan & Brenner, and his was the first *Dr. Dolittle* album, other than the original-score recording, to be finished. Before leaving for Princess Grace's annual Red Cross gala in Monte Carlo, Darin met with his press agent, Paul Bloch, of the Rogers, Cowan & Brenner office. The following day Bloch prepared a memorandum:

TO: Warren Cowan
FROM: Paul Bloch
RE: Bobby Darin

On the way to the airport last night, Bobby Darin outlined to me a plan which he wants our office to undertake, which is as follows:

We are to send his *Dr. Dolittle* album to the following list. Each album is to be accompanied by a note from Bobby Darin saying compliments of Bobby Darin. The stationery should be small and is to show the Darin finger-snapping emblem. The list is:

100 top directors	50 top TV directors **and**
100 top producers	producers
100 top actors	Army Archerd
100 writers	Jack Bradford
All personnel at CMA	Abe Greenberg
All personnel at RC&B	Harrison Carroll
Jack & Sally Hanson	Charles Champlin
Larry & Suzanne Turman	Rona Barrett
Peter & Mary Stone	Ralph Pearl
Tom & Barbara	Forrest Duke
Tannenbaum	Earl Wilson
Steve Blauner	Walter Winchell
Jackie & Barbara Cooper	Bob Ellison
Sam Peckinpah	Dorothy Manners
Dick Serafian	Tichi Miles
Jack Olensky	Sybil & Jordan
Quincy Jones	Christopher
Hank & Ginny	Roddy McDowall
Mancini	Sugar Ray Robinson
Nancy Sinatra, Sr.	Muhammad Ali
Ross Hunter	Murray Deutsch
Bob & Goldie Arthur	Key Broadway producers
Susan Stein	Maurice Landsberg
Mike Frankovich	Dick Lane (Tahoe)
Mervyn & Kitty Leroy	Doug Buchhauser (**Tahoe**)
Heads of all the studios	Bill Harrah

6

Pizazz—that's a show business word,

Gene Kelly said

Richard Zanuck signed a letter, glanced at a memorandum before throwing it into the wastebasket, then stood up as director Fred Zinnemann and producer David Weisbart walked into his office. They exchanged amenities about their recent travels and then settled down to business. The Studio had signed Zinnemann to direct a $10 million Western based on Custer's last stand and had assigned the picture to Weisbart's schedule. It was Zinnemann's first Western since he won an Academy Award for his direction of *High Noon* and he was excited about the project. Richard Zanuck's enthusiasm, however, was beginning to wane; the picture posed enormous casting and production difficulties and the huge budget, which had been honed to the bone, was causing second thoughts.

"I don't see this as a star picture," Zanuck said. "No names over the title. There isn't an actor around who can bring in enough tickets for a picture this size. Except maybe, in something like this, John Wayne."

"Not a chance," Weisbart said. He was a handsome, impeccably dressed man in his early fifties who had been a staff producer at the Studio ever since the Zanucks had regained control. "The Duke hates Custer like the plague. He thinks the whole incident is an American disgrace."

"I guess he would at that," Zanuck said.

"Let me show you some English faces," Zinnemann said, digging into a portfolio of photographs. He was a slight, pipe-smoking man with half-glasses and a soft Austrian accent. "Our concept is a newsreel of the period. If we get these English actors, we raise the whole tone of the acting and break up the clichés of Western acting."

Zanuck pored over the pictures, occasionally taking one out and laying it aside.

"I've been thinking about using cameos," Weisbart said.

Zanuck looked up quickly.

"I think it would add something to the picture to have name actors do bits," Weisbart continued.

Zanuck rose from his desk and began pacing the room, shooting his cuffs. "If we use cameos, they've got to have something to do," he said. "They've got to play roles. What I don't want is something like *The Greatest Story Ever Told*, some star coming out in butler suit saying, 'This truly was the Son of God.' "

"And that's all he has to do," Weisbart said.

"Exactly," Zanuck said.

"We won't have that in this picture," Weisbart said.

Zinnemann closed his portfolio, patting the photographs into place so that there were no white edges showing. "Is it true, Dick," he said carefully, "that you're thinking of shooting locations in Mexico?"

Zanuck nodded slowly.

"It's outrageous," Zinnemann said. "Shooting a great American folk legend in a foreign country."

"It'll save three million dollars," Zanuck replied pleasantly. "It's a factor, it's a real factor."

Zinnemann yielded the point grudgingly. He went on to the next item on his agenda. He had already won assent from the Studio to cast Toshiro Mifune, the Japanese film star, in the role of Crazy Horse, and now suggested that another Oriental play Sitting Bull. "It'll maintain an ethnic balance, Dick," Zinnemann said.

A stricken look crossed Zanuck's face. "Jesus, Freddy," he said, "you want us ostracized by the American Indian Association? Those are the two biggest heroes in the history of Indians. And you want Japs to play both of them?"

NO WONDER HUMANS CAN'T GET JOBS

In the past 12 months, there were 19,692 animal jobs in films, according to Harold Melniker, director of the American Humane Association's Hollywood office. [The AHA is responsible for supervising animals in films.]

The animal most frequently cast was the horse, with 12,464 jobs for them. In a significant first, sheep topped cattle with 2,593 of the woolies facing the shutters and only 2,181 cows working. In 1967, it was in reverse, with 2,200 cows versus 193 sheep.

Least popular among species used in pix are hawks, mice, storks, pelicans, jackals, springhauses, anteaters and apes. According to Melniker, "It's not because they can't act as well as other animals—but only because they're not as popular with film writers."

The Hollywood Reporter

Besides *Dr. Dolittle* and *Star!*, the Studio had two other major roadshow pictures in preparation, *Hello, Dolly!* and *Tom Swift*. The latter was a camp spectacular based on the boys' adventure stories by Victor Appleton. A first-draft script had been written and Gene Kelly, the dancer, had been assigned to direct. Though the picture was not yet locked in on the production schedule, the art department was hard at work making preliminary designs of Tom Swift's aeroship. The actual construction of the aeroship was to be undertaken by the Boeing Aircraft Corporation. Late in the summer, Kelly and *Tom Swift*'s producer, Frank McCarthy, arranged to have Jerry Reynolds, the Boeing engineer in charge of the project, flown to Los Angeles to discuss whether the preliminary designs were aerodynamically feasible. The meeting took place in the office of *Tom Swift*'s art director, Dale Hennesy. The walls of Hennesy's office were covered with old rotogravures of dirigibles and antique airplanes, and hanging from a fluorescent light was a paper model of the proposed airship. Reynolds seemed notably out of place among the half dozen casually attired people crammed in Hennesy's small office. He was wearing a salt-and-pepper sport jacket and perforated shoes and he nervously kept wiping the lenses of his rimless glasses with a handkerchief.

Kelly was late, and while the group waited for him to arrive, Jerry Reynolds poked at the sausage-shaped aeroship with a pencil. The plan was to have the lighter-than-air craft suspended by cables from a helicopter when it was actually flying. For the air shots, Kelly and his camera crew would film from another helicopter. At last, Kelly breezed into the office. He was wearing a sport shirt and a plaid golf cap. He sailed the golf cap across the room onto a couch. He was not wearing his toupee and Reynolds seemed startled at seeing him without hair.

"Well, Mr. Reynolds . . . what's your first name, by the way?" Kelly said.

"Jerry," Reynolds said.

"Well, Jerry," Kelly said, pointing to the model, "all I want to know is, will it work?"

"Yes, sir, it will work," Reynolds said.

Kelly smiled the smile that had lit several score pictures. "Then I guess I can go back to my office," he said.

Reynolds looked perplexed. "Well, there are certain aerodynamic problems . . ."

"I'm sure there are, Jerry," Kelly said soothingly. "But let me tell you what we want and then you can tell us what you can do." Again the smile. "Okay?"

Reynolds nodded solemnly.

"First of all, Jerry, we want an exciting visual concept," Kelly said. "That means a lot of gimmickry and pizazz—that's a show business word—on the space ship. This picture is about Tom Swift and his aeroship, and if we have an aeroship that looks like an uncooked hot dog, well, I know I don't have to tell you, Jerry, we don't have a picture. So I want all maximum gimmickry"—he nodded reassuringly—"that will be aero-dynamically feasible, of course."

Reynolds studied the model. "It will mean more money, of course, these, uh, gimmicks," he said. "And the round shape you've got now is unstable. But we can put some aerodynamic tricks on it."

"Great, Jerry," Kelly said. "We put our tricks on it and you put your tricks on it and we're in business."

"I would say that, sir," Reynolds said.

"Now what about the chopper?" Kelly said. "Will the prop wash make the aeroship swing and sway like Sammy Kaye?"

"Sammy Kaye," Reynolds said uncertainly. Then he smiled broadly. "Sammy Kaye. Well, I think we can make allowances."

"A fun-looking design," Kelly said. "You get me."

"I get you," Reynolds said. He peered at the model. "What's the maximum altitude you want to fly at?"

"12,000 feet," Kelly said.

Reynolds exhaled. "That might be a problem. How many people will you have in the aeroship?"

"Five," Kelly said. "But not at 12,000. We'll use dummies at that height. I wouldn't even ask a stunt man to go aboard at 12,000."

Reynolds fingered a slide rule. "The slower this, uh, aeroship goes, the simpler our problem becomes," he said. "What I need from you is the minimum speed you can function at."

"We have to get a feeling of motion," Hennesy said.

"Absolutely," Kelly said.

"Well, 80 knots at 3,000 feet looks like you're scarcely moving."

"Like still shots," Kelly said. He was twirling his golf cap around on his finger.

"So you need speeds . . ." Reynolds began.

". . . that will give the cinematographer full amplitude," Kelly interrupted. Reynolds nodded. He began making rapid calculations on a scratch pad.

"Maybe we can do wind-tunnel tests," Kelly suggested.

"No, sir, I don't think so," Reynolds said. "Our studies will be accurate enough."

"I trust you implicitly, Jerry," Kelly said. "Just one last thing. When we bring the aeroship down after a shot, will there be much of a jolt?"

"It will be like going over a bump in a road," Reynolds said.

"You don't know *ac*-tors, Jerry," Kelly said. "We jolt them two or three times, it doesn't help my relations with them."

"I can understand that," Reynolds said.

Kelly rose and patted the golf cap onto his head. "The more this aeroship looks like Tom Swift built it in his garage and not Boeing Vertol, the happier I'll be." He shook Reynolds' hand. "Ready when you are, C.B.," Kelly said.

Though *Planet of the Apes* was not finished shooting, a trailer for theater preview had been prepared and was ready for Arthur Jacobs' inspection. He sagged into a seat in the Studio Theater and motioned Mort Abrahams to tell the projectionist he was ready. The film showed Maurice Evans, Roddy McDowall, Kim Hunter and James Daly in normal contemporary clothes and then dissolved into a shot of each in ape makeup. The last shot was of Linda Harrison, a Fox contract player who was playing Nova, The Earth Girl, one of the human captives of the apes. As her picture flickered on the screen, Jacobs sat bolt upright in his chair.

"Who the hell made her up?" he said. "Jesus, what a lousy makeup job."

"She's not wearing any eye shadow," Abrahams said. "And that dye job on her hair. It looks like it was done with black shoe polish."

Jacobs switched on the light by his seat. "Call Ben Nye and tell him to take a look at this." Nye was the head of the Studio makeup department. "That's the cheapest lipstick I ever saw."

"She's not playing Anna Christie, for Christ's sake," Abrahams said.

"Tell Ben Nye I want him to make her up himself," Jacobs said. "We'll reshoot on Monday."

Later that afternoon, the sketches for the main title design of *Planet of the Apes* were delivered to Jacobs, and he and Abrahams drove over to Stage 9 to show them to the film's director, Franklin Schaffner. The designer of the titles was a young man named Don Record, who had also designed the main title of *Dr. Dolittle*. He was wearing a bright red shirt and plaid mod pants with a wide leather belt. Record's first renderings of the *Planet of the Apes* titles had been rejected by Schaffner, who thought them too mechanical and realistic. It was only in the titles that the actual space trip of Charlton Heston and his fellow astronauts would be seen, and Schaffner wanted to hold back the surprise that the spacecraft had crashed through the time barrier.

Schaffner was talking to Heston outside the latter's dressing room when Jacobs, Abrahams and Record strolled onto the set.

"Jesus," Jacobs whispered to Abrahams, "don't tell Chuck we've got the sketches. We're going to have enough trouble satisfying Frank." He raised his arm in greeting to Heston. "*Salud.*"

"*Salud*, Arthur," Heston said.

"The dailies look great, Chuck," Jacobs said.

"I think we've got something more than mere entertainment here," Heston said.

"Jesus, as long as it's not a message picture," Jacobs said nervously.

"We've got entertainment *and* a message in this picture, Arthur," Heston said.

"Great," Jacobs said.

Schaffner lit a thin cigar and walked back toward his trailer. He is a wary, edgy man in his late forties who had made his reputation in live television. His trailer was sparsely furnished with a plaid couch, a desk and a bulletin board, on which Record set the title sketches. He explained that he had tried to overcome Schaffner's previous objections by keeping the realistic effects in the background and using optical effects, montages and changes of color to suggest the passage of time. Schaffner was still not impressed.

"In the first place, we're supposed to show the people aging," he said. He tapped one of the sketches. "Well, we've got a hand insert here, but the guy's fingernails haven't grown any longer. And will we show him growing a beard?"

"Good point," Jacobs said.

"I think it's too overwhelmingly technical," Schaffner

said. He examined the sketches intently. "Look, we're telegraphing to the audience that the space ship is going through the time barrier. There's one, two, three, four shots of the computer clock going from 1968 here to the year 3250 in the last one. I want to set that up dramatically, not in the titles like you've got it here."

"A point," Jacobs said.

"But, Frank, so what if the audience knows, the crew doesn't," Abrahams said.

"My point is that we're robbing the audience of a surprise," Schaffner said, biting each word off carefully. "I don't want to telegraph it. I want to set it up in dialogue. I think that's reasonable enough to ask."

"Right," Jacobs said. "The important thing is the picture, not the titles."

"As I understand it, you want to extend the space trip because the only time we see it is during the titles," Schaffner said. "Right?"

Jacobs nodded in agreement. "And to show the concept of time, of separation, of the shattering loneliness."

Schaffner deliberately ground out his cigar. "Well, these titles don't sell that concept to me. Now how are we going to show that concept, realistically or abstractly?"

"I guess abstractly," Jacobs said tentatively.

"Is it possible," Schaffner said, turning to Record, "to use black-and-white as well as color?"

Record nodded.

"Let's try that then," Schaffner said. He touched Jacobs on the arm and walked out toward the set.

"You've got the idea, Don, right?" Abrahams said.

"We're agreed we want to show the separation, loneliness and the passage of time."

"Abstractly," Jacobs said.

As a publicity tie-in for *The Sweet Ride,* Joe Pasternak had agreed to give a small walk-on in the picture to a Las Vegas showgirl who had won the title of "Miss Talent International." "We won't get much space out of it," said Milt Smith, the Studio publicity man assigned to *The Sweet Ride.* "But every little bit helps." Several days after the stunt was agreed upon, Smith walked disgustedly into his office. "You know that slob with the boobs?" he said. " 'Miss Talent International' she calls herself—how do you like that? Well, she's making a hundred and a half a week in Vegas, but you know what she wants? Five hundred a week net. For waving her knockers in front of the camera. So Joe says, 'Tell her to go fuck herself.' "

A conversation with Joan Baez is a crash course on rudeness. I discovered that as a fellow guest on a segment of the Donald O'Connor Show. Miss Baez, close-cropped, had chopped off her locks the week before. It was an act of defiance, I suppose: she said she doesn't think an entertainer should have a trademark, or mannerisms. In that case, Miss Baez should study her manners. Throughout the talk, she proved that her words, like her tax returns, won't stand up under analysis. She delivered a lot of drivel on Vietnam, weaponry, the need for "caring" and for changing our political system. "What do you think of Mr. Nixon?" asked her host. "You discuss Nixon," she snapped. "I have never voted. I never will." Miss Baez must consider that smart. I consider it irresponsible. She has a beautiful singing voice, but her style hasn't matured anymore than her comportment. She is miles behind the really hip young people of today.

On a program whose guests included David Janssen and a swinging twosome, the Avant Garde, she even made Donald O'Connor lose his cool. "What shall we talk about!" he asked Miss Baez.

"You have a list of questions there. Ask them."

"Okay, baby, you want to be asked, I'll ask you," Donald said. "How does it feel to be up the river?"

Joyce Haber, The Los Angeles Times

Richard Zanuck took his place at the head of his private luncheon table in a small, tree-guarded alcove outside the Studio commissary. A portable awning protected one end of the table from the hot summer sun, but Zanuck, who is a health enthusiast, sat in its glare. On his plate, as there was every day, was a piece of paper listing the closing price of Fox stock on the New York Stock Exchange and the number of shares traded. The closing price that day was 55¼ and the volume traded was 17,000 shares.

"Down an eighth," Stan Hough said. Hough is one of the four people who lunch with Zanuck every day, the other three being Harry Sokolov, Owen McLean and Doc Merman. There were three other places at the table for favored Studio employees and guests. Hough passed the market information down the table, and the conversation turned to a scandal that had just broken in the papers that week about high-stakes gambling at the Friars Club, a private club in Beverly Hills whose members were largely connected with show business. According to the reports, a few of the club's members enticed other Friars and outsiders into rigged gin-rummy games. Some of the losers had been taken for $200,000 and $300,000, and a number of such eminent show business figures as Phil Silvers and Tony Martin had been subpoenaed to testify before a federal grand jury investigating the case in Los Angeles. Doc Merman was a Friars member, and as he explained how the games were fixed, an agent named Kurt Frings appeared at the table.

"I got the big news," Frings said. He was a large, red-faced man with a thick German accent. "I got subpoenaed this morning."

"Are you a victim, Kurt, or were you a winner?" Harry Sokolov said.

Frings made an obscene gesture toward Sokolov. "I'm not even a member," he said. "I play there twice. On a Saturday and a Sunday afternoon. Two days, I didn't even go down once. Not once."

"How much did you lose?" Zanuck said.

Frings threw up his hands. "I made a deal," he said. "I don't want the publicity. I said I'd talk if they don't mention the money I lose."

Zanuck cut into a shrimp. "I heard they were only subpoenaing people who tapped out for fifty grand, Kurt."

Frings moved his shoulders expressively.

"Two afternoons, you must have been good for a hundred anyway," Merman said.

"Please, I don't want to mention the money," Frings said. "You know how they did it? They brought in a guy from out of state to bug the place."

"That's what brought the Feds in," Sokolov said. "You bring a guy in from out of state to put a bug in and you've got the FBI on your hands."

"They had a peephole in the ceiling," Frings said. He

had ordered lox and capers and a caper had stuck to the corner of his mouth. His face was wreathed with sweat. "The guy up in the ceiling had some kind of magnifying glass set up so he could see the whole table. And the guy playing who was in on the fix had some kind of buzzer system around his waist. Say the pigeon had two kings and the other guy was going to drop a king. The guy in the ceiling would give him a little jolt with the buzzer. Two for drop, one for don't drop, I don't know, but it worked. They took Tony Martin for a hundred grand, I hear. Anyway, the guy would get the jolt, stick his king back and drop something else."

"The guy upstairs must have been a good gin player," Zanuck said.

"I hear they pay him $200 a day," Frings said.

"What I don't understand is who blew the whistle," Hough said.

"The wives," Merman said, slowly sipping a cup of coffee. "The wives squawked. A guy comes home and tells his wife he dropped fifty grand playing gin, it's a big thing."

Several months before, the Studio had finished shooting on *Valley of the Dolls*, a relatively inexpensive nonroadshow production based on Jacqueline Susann's bestselling novel and produced by David Weisbart and Mark Robson (the latter had also directed the film). By midsummer, while the picture was being scored and edited, a major publicity campaign was already underway, for the Studio expected *Valley of the Dolls* to be its principal soft-ticket attraction during the winter months. One morning late in July, Frank Neill, a chunky, beet-faced man who was the assistant director of Hollywood publicity, walked into the office of Lou Dyer, another Studio press agent. Chewing on an unlit cigar, he went to the bookcase and took out a copy of *The Motion Picture Almanac*. He sat heavily on the couch and began flipping through it. His finger ran down a page and then stopped. "David Weisbart," Neill said softly.

"What about him?" Dyer said.

"He just dropped dead," Neill said. "He was playing golf with Mark Robson. Just keeled over."

"What hole?" Dyer said.

"I don't know," Neill said. "Take care of it, will you, Lou? Get hold of the *Times* and the *Examiner*. We've got enough time for the trades."

"The wire services will pick it up from the papers," Dyer said.

"Right," Neill said. He spat out a piece of the cigar. "It was at the Brentwood Country Club."

Dyer picked up the telephone, dialed the Brentwood Country Club and asked for the manager. He identified himself and explained that he was checking on the circumstances of Weisbart's death. "What is your name, sir?" Dyer said. "Mr. Gill." He reached for a pencil and began taking notes. "With Mark Robson, yes, I have that. He's the director. Was it a twosome or a foursome? Just a twosome. I see. And what hole was he on? Or had he just teed off? The tenth? Fine. Well, thank you, Mr. Gill." He checked his notes. "Oh, one thing. What is your first name? For the papers, that's right. And you are the manager. Thank you, Mr. Gill, thank you very much."

Neill came back into the office with some photographs of Weisbart and a canned Studio biography of the producer. "I think we can still make the first editions," Neill said. "We'll send a bag downtown. And, Lou, when you call the papers, don't forget to say that Robson had co-producer status on the picture."

Dyer dialed again and got the city desk of the *Los Angeles Times*. He quickly explained the circumstances of Weisbart's death to the desk man on the other end of the line. "A messenger is coming down with a bio," he said. "But let me give you a couple of his hits. He produced *Kid Galahad, Our Miss Brooks, Rebel Without a Cause*—that's the picture that zoomed James Dean to stardom. He started out as a film editor working with such film greats as Michael Curtiz." Dyer paused. "Curtiz. That's C for Charlie, U, R, T for Tom, I, Z for zebra."

7

It transcends business, Irving,

David Brown said

As the script for *The Boston Strangler* neared completion, director Richard Fleischer and producer Robert Fryer flew back and forth to Boston scouting exterior and necessary interior locations. At the Studio, Stan Hough's production department worked out the final details of the budget. When he was in Los Angeles, Fryer spent hours every day in a Studio projection room looking at footage of actors being considered for parts in *The Boston Strangler*. A few days after Edward Anhalt turned in the final draft of his screenplay, the script was mimeographed and distributed to all the Studio department heads so that they could make a final estimate of the costs their departments would incur on the picture. The correlation of the below-the-line costs was overseen by Hough and Doc Merman. One Thursday afternoon Merman called the *Strangler* production staff and the Studio department heads together for a final budget meeting.

The meeting took place in the conference room of the production bungalow. Fryer, Fleischer and Merman sat at the head of the T-shaped conference table and the rest of the thirty or so conferees sat down on either side of the table. Everyone in the room was given a mimeographed production breakdown of each of *The Boston Strangler*'s 90 sequences and 256 scenes. The breakdown was titled "THE BOSTON STRANGLER—STORY 147 —PRODUCER: ROBERT FRYER—DIRECTOR: RICHARD FLEISCHER." Every sequence in the script had been broken down into its basic elements—set, location, major cast members, bit players, extras and animals (if necessary), special props, special effects and sequence plot synopsis.

Merman tapped his glasses on the table and brought the meeting to order. "The first problem," he said, "is what is the last year in the time sequence of the story?"

"1964," Fleischer said.

"So in any street scenes, we can't have cars later than 1964 models," Merman said. "Right?"

"Right," Fleischer said.

"And they weren't wearing miniskirts in 1964," Merman said. "So we're going to have to watch that in the crowd scenes."

Fleischer nodded.

Merman went through the breakdown page by page. Occasionally there was a discussion of potential problems within the individual sequences:

PAGE NO. 7
SET: INT/EXT POLICE CAR—PARKING LOT OF BAR
LOCATION: STUDIO
CAST: JOE
BITS: CLOE
SPECIAL PROPS: POLICE CAR, AUTOS FOR PARKING LOT, NEWSPAPER
SYNOPSIS: CLOE INFORMS JOE OF CARR'S STRANGE SEX HABITS

"Let's do that right here at the Studio on the French street," Fleischer said.

"There's not enough room there for a parking lot," Merman said.

Fleischer folded his hands on the table in front of him. He stared straight ahead, quiet, almost dreamlike, not looking at Merman. "It doesn't have to be a parking lot," he said. "We can dress the French street to make it look like a Boston alley."

PAGE NO. 9
SET: INT HOMICIDE SECTION—POLICE HEADQUARTERS
LOCATION: STUDIO
CAST: WILLIS, BRANDY, MC AFEE, JOE
BITS: NEWSMAN #1
SYNOPSIS: WILLIS DISCUSSES CRIME WITH REPORTER— ANOTHER KILLING REPORTED

"Is this going to be an exact replica of Boston Homicide?" Merman said.

Fryer shook his head. "No, they wouldn't let us in to get any pictures. The Boston cops didn't like the way they came off in the book, so they're not giving us any help."

"You should go to Boston, get yourself arrested and take pictures with a Minox, Robert," Merman said, his beagle features breaking into a grin. "Isn't that what a creative producer does?"

"Let's just build a set," Fleischer said.

"How about using the standing set we've got for *Felony Squad?*" Merman said. "It's nice and modern."

"Because it's an old police station in Boston," Fleischer said.

Merman threw up his hands. "So who knows from an old police station?"

"Me," Fleischer said.

"Okay," Merman said. "I was just trying to save you some money."

PAGE NO. 24
SET: INT ATTORNEY GENERAL'S OFFICE
LOCATION
CAST: EDWARD BROOKE, BOTTOMLY
SPECIAL PROPS: ICED TEA, SCOTCH
SYNOPSIS: BROOKE TRIES UNSUCCESSFULLY TO ENLIST
        BOTTOMLY IN INVESTIGATION

Merman blanched when he saw the scene was going to be shot on location. "It's an interior," he said. "Why not build a set and shoot it here?"

"No," Fleischer said. "You don't get the same feeling, the desk, the chairs, the mementos."

"We can take pictures," Merman said strenuously. "Duplicate it here."

"Uh-uh," Fleischer said.

"When do you expect to use this office?" Merman said. "When the attorney general's out taking a leak in the men's room?"

"On a Saturday," Fleischer said.

Merman looked down the table at Fryer for assistance. "I don't want to interfere with your creative talents, Mr. Producer, but you've got four and a half pages of dialogue in this scene," Merman said. "That's a long day's work and Mr. Director says you'll be working on Saturday. Well, I've got to remind you, Mr. Producer, Saturday is double time. You build a set here, you're saving money."

"Let's spend it," Fleischer said.

PAGE NO. 43
SET: INT BLUE FALCON BAR
LOCATION
CAST: BOTTOMLY
BITS: LAURENCE SHAW, HAROLD, CEDRIC
EXTRAS: HOMOSEXUALS (MALE, FEMALE), BARTENDERS,
   WAITERS
SPECIAL PROPS: DRINKS
SYNOPSIS: SHAW EXPLAINS TO BOTTOMLY HIS SEXUAL
   ARRANGEMENT WITH MISS RIDGEWAY—BOT-
   TOMLY SHOCKED

"Why not build that one here?" Merman said.

"I'd rather use a real location and real faggots," Fleischer said. He smiled benignly down the table at Merman.

"Well, I guess they must have a faggot bar somewhere in Boston," Merman said.

"I want to do as many interiors on location as possible," Fleischer said. "You get a better feeling, a better sense of place. If we have an interior where there's a lot of people, which means a lot of staging and a lot of camera movements, we'll do it here. You can get more control on a stage. Otherwise, if there's just a small group of people, I'd rather use the real thing on location."

PAGE NO. 50
SET: EXT PROVIDENCE AIRPORT
LOCATION
CAST: MC AFEE, BRANDY, BOTTOMLY, JOE, PETER HUR-
      KOS, JIM CRANE
EXTRAS: AIRPORT EMPLOYEES
SPECIAL PROPS: JET AIRCRAFT, POLICE CARS
SYNOPSIS: AS STAFF WAITS TO PICK UP HURKOS, MC AFEE
          BRIEFS BRANDY ON NEW SUSPECT O'BRIEN—
          THEY PICK UP HURKOS

"We'll freeze our ass off if we shoot this in Providence in the middle of winter," said Buck Hall, Fleischer's assistant director.

Fleischer nodded. "Let's use a local location," he said. "Santa Monica Airport, maybe. We can spread some snow around and make it look like winter." He stared off into space, reflecting for a moment. "What airlines fly into Providence anyway?"

"Eastern and American," Eric Stacey, the *Strangler's* unit production manager, said. "But I don't think Providence was a jet airport in 1964. So Hurkos would have had to come in on an Electra and American isn't using them anymore."

"Eastern still uses them, but Eastern doesn't fly into L.A.," the representative from the prop department said.

"That means we're going to have to find an Electra and paint it," Stacey said. "That gets expensive. It might be cheaper to shoot the scene in Providence."

Everyone at the table looked at Fleischer. He shook

his head slowly. "Negative," he said finally. "We use all the same actors in the next scene in the Providence motel room. That's a set we're building here at the Studio. If we shoot the airport scene in Providence, we've got to keep all the actors on the payroll until we fly them out here for the motel room scene. And *that* gets expensive. So let's find an Electra—I think Western uses them—paint it and use one of the local airports."

PAGE NO. 68
SET: EXT STREET IN FRONT OF TAYLOR'S APARTMENT
LOCATION
CAST: ALBERT, MR. TAYLOR
BITS: POLICEMEN (2), STUNTMAN FOR FALL?
EXTRAS: PEDESTRIANS, MOTORISTS (30)
SPECIAL PROPS: POLICE CAR
SYNOPSIS: ALBERT RUNS THROUGH STREETS, ALLEYS,
        ETC., PURSUED BY POLICE AND MR. TAYLOR—
        IS FINALLY CAPTURED

Fleischer tapped the breakdown with a pencil. "What do you mean only thirty extras, Doc?" he said impatiently. "This is a main city thoroughfare and the shot covers two blocks. Are you trying to tell me that in the middle of the day in Boston you're only going to find thirty people on the street? Come on, Doc. We need 130 extras anyway, and even that's not enough. Make it 150."

PAGE NO. 80
SET: EXT FRONT OF STATLER AND DEPARTMENT STORE
        WINDOW
LOCATION
CAST: ALBERT, ANNA SLESERS

EXTRAS: PARADE SPECTATORS—MEN, WOMEN
SPECIAL PROPS: CARS
SYNOPSIS: ALBERT RE-CREATES SEEING ANNA SLESERS—
    FOLLOWING HER—GOING THROUGH STORE
    WINDOW AFTER HER

Fleischer pressed his hands against his temples. "I think we've got to shoot that here," he said. "You set up outside a department store at midday, you've got a madhouse. We need control." He thought for a moment. "How about using the New York street at Metro?"

"That's $6,000 a day," Merman said. "Are you sure you can't shoot it in Boston?"

"Sure I can shoot it, Doc," Fleischer said. "But you start tying up a main drag, it will take four weeks to shoot."

"If we're going to spend $6,000 a day, I'd rather build a set here," Merman said.

"Sure, if you can do it, fine," Fleischer said. "I'm not in love with the idea of giving Metro money. But let's keep the idea on the back burner."

Late one afternoon, Richard Zanuck received a telephone call from Governor Ronald Reagan's office in Sacramento. The caller was one of Reagan's aides, who wondered if the Studio had a spare lawyer it could lend the administration to help out in the utilities commission during the summer holidays. Zanuck listened politely to the caller and said he would get back to him. When he hung up, he rang Harry Sokolov.

"Ronnie Reagan wants to borrow a lawyer," Zanuck said. "They're short-handed in Sacramento with everyone taking vacations up there. Check the legal department and see if we can spare one, and if we can, let's throw him one for four weeks. It never hurts to have a friend in Sacramento."

Paul Monash was having trouble finding stories for his new television series, *Judd*. It was Monash's hope that his lawyer hero would each week become enmeshed in a controversial case that involved a certain amount of social commentary. The difficulty lay in the fact that *Judd* still had not premiered on the air and so was unproved in the ratings; until it was proved, the amount of controversy was limited, and a crusading lawyer without controversy was a peculiarly bloodless anomaly. It was during this limbo stage that Monash met late one afternoon with a writer named William Froug, who himself had produced a crusading liberal lawyer series, *Sam Benedict*, for another studio several years before. A casual, slightly puffy man in his late forties, Froug had an idea for a *Judd* segment that he wanted to discuss with Monash. (Under the rules of the Writers Guild of America West, a member of the television branch cannot put one word on paper without being paid for it; the usual procedure is for the Guild member to talk over an idea with a producer, and if the producer likes the idea, the writer is given a monetary commitment and told to go ahead.)

Monash adjusted the air conditioner to high, opened a diet soda, shucked off his shoes and nestled into the chair. "Shoot," he said.

"Support your local police," Froug said.

Monash arched an eyebrow. "That's your *story*?"

"An ironic twist off it," Froug said. "We've got this editor in Texas . . ."

"Does it have to be in Texas?" Monash asked.

"No."

"Then let's put him someplace else," Monash said, tucking his legs beneath him. "Texas is too easy."

"Sure," Froug said. "No problem." He unbuttoned his Madras jacket. He had an even *café-au-lait* colored tan. "Anyway, this editor writes an editorial saying the local chief of police is a sadist. He beat up a suspect in jail or something. The suspect is a kid involved in a mugging, something like that, and our cop let him have it. He maybe even murdered the kid."

Monash sucked on the soda bottle. "Why's the editor write the editorial?" he said.

"Because he wants a libel suit," Froug said. "He knows the cop will sue him for libel, and he figures if he can get Judd as his defense attorney, Judd can break down the cop in court and prove he was a murderer."

"I don't get the chief's dilemma," Monash said. He knotted his hands behind his head and stared at the ceiling, considering the story.

"You mean the turn in the middle?" Froug said.

"Mmmmm," Monash mused. "I mean what makes the chief a sadist. Maybe there's some kind of venal reason." He kept examining the ceiling. "And I don't think your editor works. Editors are too careful about libel."

There was silence in the office as both Monash and Froug contemplated alternative plot possibilities. The only sound was the whirring of the air conditioner.

"How about this?" Monash said finally. "How about a letter to the paper? The editor can publish a disclaimer, 'the views in the letters column are not the views of the paper,' some bullshit like that. You see, the editor covers himself, but at the same time he has some inside information he wants out in the open. So he gets a citizen with status in the community to write the letter."

"Someone with clout," Froug said.

"Now we need a little motivation," Monash said. He began snapping his fingers. "Why does a guy get hot pants to get the chief?" He thought for a moment. "Maybe he just wants the excitement."

Froug looked doubtful.

"Look," Monash said, "part of the reason I went to the peace march in Century City was because I thought it was going to be exciting. Sure, it mirrored my views, I think the Vietnam war is shit, but I thought I'd get a little jazz out of the march, too." He stared somewhat enviously at Froug. "You were there, weren't you beaten up?"

"No, I was just ducking blows," Froug said. "Quite frankly, that's how I came up with this idea."

"Con-tro-ver-sy," Monash said. He laughed disparagingly.

"That's right," Froug said. "I know you want controversial subjects for *Judd*. Well, you got one in police brutality." He brightened suddenly. "We could even have a demonstration in this story."

Monash seemed resigned. "What in TV terms would be an acceptable demonstration?" he said. "We can't have a peace march, we know that."

"The only acceptable demonstration in television land is against stamping on dogs," Froug said.

"I've got it," Monash said suddenly. "Who says we've got to say what kind of demonstration? What if we never said what the demonstration was all about? What if we just let the audience fill it in in their own minds?"

Froug considered that. "What about a love-in?" he countered. "I'm very interested in kids. I'm executive director of Community Action for Fact and Freedom and we helped negotiate peace on the Sunset Strip when the kids rioted up there."

Monash shook his head. "The problem with a love-in is that it's not mobile enough in camera terms. Look, we don't have to say the Century Plaza, but that's what it's all about."

"Okay," Froug said.

"And we've got to make the situation with the police chief more venal. Someone should have his hand in the till. We need a crime, because I don't think the demonstration will fill out much in terms of plot. You get a crime, you get some pressures between Judd and the principals. And a crime works in the mytholand of TV." Monash ran his fingers around the neck of his turtleneck sweater. "We might even have Judd lose this one."

"Has he lost one yet?" Froug said.

Monash shook his head. "No, but I think the time has come. We can't have every case turn on, 'Yes, Mrs. Mazurki, but is this the prescription for your glasses?' "

Froug laughed. "The name of the game today is race riots and police brutality and we're sitting here doing stories on crooked cops."

"Don't fight it." Monash shrugged. "There's one more thing. You got any good stories left over from your *Sam Benedict* days that we could steal? We're hurting."

"Sure, no problem," Froug said. The suggestion did not seem to surprise him.

"You got any, we'll disguise them," Monash said. "Change a him to her, a gun to a knife, you know. But we are really hard up for stories. I just bootlegged a copy of a *Defenders* script on the M'Naghten Rule to see how they handled it."

"What's mine is yours," Froug said. He stood up and yawned. "I'll go through the files to see what I have and then I'll call you in a couple of days about the editor and the police chief."

RIOTING HALTS "MAYA"
Srinigar, Kashmir—Street rioting between Hindus and Moslems, now in its third week in this northern India capital, has halted production of the King Brothers, MGM-TV series, "Maya."

The Hollywood Reporter .

As the summer wore on, the Studio was more and more convinced that in *Valley of the Dolls*, which was still being scored and edited, it had its biggest non-roadshow grosser since *Peyton Place*. In its preliminary estimates, the Studio's sales department predicted a gross of $20 million. The record hard- and soft-cover sales of *Valley of the Dolls* had made its author, Jacqueline Susann, a celebrity in her own right. So sanguine was the Studio about the box office prospects of *Dolls* that it was anxious to capitalize on the author's celebrity by tying up the film rights for her unfinished new novel, *The Love Machine*. Jacqueline Susann's business affairs were overseen by her husband, a shrewd former television producer named Irving Mansfield, who had a genius for promoting his wife, *Valley of the Dolls* and *The Love Machine*, in whatever order the circumstances dictated. The unprecedented success of *Dolls* had been as much a surprise to the Mansfields as to anyone else, and they were slightly perturbed that they had let the film rights of the book go to the Studio for relatively so little money—$85,000 down with an escalation clause that brought the final price up to $200,-000. The Mansfields were convinced that if they had waited until the book had climbed to the top of the best-seller lists, they could have received a minimum of $450,000, along with a share of the film's profits. With this experience in mind, they were determined not to let *The Love Machine* go for anything less than top dollar. Though Jacqueline Susann did not yet have a completion date for her new book, Fox was already jockeying to see the manuscript before any other studio in Hollywood, and was willing to pay handsomely for the privilege. One morning David Brown, the Studio's vice president in charge of story operations, called George Chasin, Jacqueline Susann's West Coast agent, and sounded him out on the possibility of Fox's getting first look at *The Love Machine*. Brown's inducement was $125,000. Rather than going directly to Jacqueline Susann, this sum would be paid to Mansfield to produce a picture mutually acceptable to himself and the Studio. If on the basis of its first look, Fox subsequently bought *The Love Machine*, Mansfield would receive an additional $125,000 to produce this picture also. The Studio's offer of a quarter of a million dollars to Mansfield was only a sweetener; it would not be applied to the ultimate purchase price of *The Love Machine* (a figure estimated as high as $1 million). As a final lollipop, Brown told Chasin that if the Studio bought the book, it would also cut the Mansfields in on 5 per cent of the film profits on *Valley of the Dolls*.

"There's not another studio in a position to make that kind of offer, George," Brown said, sucking on his pipe. "We think *Dolls* is going to be a big one."

When Brown hung up the telephone, he brooded for a moment, tamping down the tobacco in the bowl of his pipe with a book of matches. "Agents are so noncommittal," he said finally. "He said he'd think about it and get back to us."

Brown rang for his secretary and asked her to get Irving Mansfield at the Beverly Hills Hotel. The Mansfields were scheduled to leave for New York within the hour.

"Irving," Brown said, when Mansfield came on the phone. "I just wanted to say safe trip. It was good seeing you, Irving. It's always good seeing you and Jackie." He leaned back in his chair and let a puff of smoke curl toward the ceiling. "I just talked to George Chasin, Irving, and made a little proposal to him. I'm sure he'll be getting in touch with you. Well, have a good trip back, and Helen and I will get together with you and Jackie in New York. Friends, Irving, friends. It transcends business, Irving."

Several days later, Owen McLean and Jack Baur walked over to Stage 2 where the New Talent Program was headquartered. They were scheduled to watch a young neophyte actress test for the program. The Studio had started the talent school in the chimerical hope that a roster of contract players could reverse the spiraling demands of the major independent stars. Talent scouts combed the U.S. looking for faces and figures. There were approximately twenty-five applicants to the school every week, and of these the Studio auditioned five and selected one. The chosen were signed to an exclusive long-term contract; the initial salary was $175 a week, and at the beginning of the contract, there were options every six months. Once accepted, the students attended classes on voice, dancing, mime, action and acting techniques. The school was run by Pamela Danova, a diva-shaped European actress and voice teacher, and Curt Conway, a veteran Broadway actor, but responsibility for final selection to the school rested with McLean and Baur.

By the door of the stage was a sign that said, "Remember, An Actor Killed Lincoln," and on the bulletin board a stern instruction sheet prepared by Pamela Danova and given to each new student:

WHAT IS EXPECTED OF YOU

The image of the star is what has made Hollywood great. You will reflect that image constantly, whether at the studio or shopping for groceries. You are being groomed for stardom in every possible way. That means you must be a master of your craft, be able to walk with poise, speak with assurance and clarity, and behave with propriety. You will learn to be gracious to anyone and everyone in preparation for the day when you yourself will have fans and admirers of your own. The time has passed for stars to resemble the boy and girl next door or the beatniks. When someone pays money to go to the movies, they expect to see handsome, clean-looking young people—not slovenly, mumbling, scratching delinquents. You will dress properly. That means no more sweatshirts, sweaters and blue jeans. No more straggly hair, slacks and sneakers. Contract players adjudged to be lazy, untidy or undisciplined will be eliminated from the Studio Roster.

The stage was bare save for a few props. McLean and Baur took chairs between Conway and Pamela Danova.

The girl being tested had worked up a scene from *Breakfast at Tiffany's*. She was a pert young thing in an orange miniskirt and matching orange arm bracelets. The actor appearing in the scene with her was already a member of the program. He was wearing chino pants and an open-necked button-down shirt. The girl sat on the prop couch, her legs hiked up underneath her. The actor did not have much to do in the scene, but he had been in the school long enough to know how to upstage the girl. He prowled behind her on the couch, where she couldn't see him, picking up things, patting his hair, leaning on a chair almost as if he were doing pushups. The girl knew something was going on behind her, but she could not destroy the mood of the scene and look back. She played with her arm bracelet and ad-libbed a giggle after one of his lines. When the scene was over, she reached back over the couch and with a large smile squeezed the actor's hand.

"Cute scene," Baur said.

"But I couldn't hear you," McLean said to the girl.

She smiled nervously. Then she giggled. "I've got a little voice."

McLean chewed on his eyeglasses noncommittally. "Thanks, kids," he said.

The girl lingered before she left the room, adjusting her arm bracelets, flipping idly through a script that someone had left lying around. No one spoke and finally she left.

"She won't photograph well," McLean said.

"Didn't you think she had a certain . . . gamine charm?" Pamela Danova said.

"From a certain angle, she's got lousy teeth," McLean

said. "But I liked the boy. He's a strange-looking kid. A lot of balls. He looks like he might be dangerous."

"Unfortunately, acting ability is not the primary requirement for pictures," Curt Conway said a few afternoons later. He has long gray hair and he was inhaling deeply on a cigarette. The New Talent contractees were all in tights, bathed in sweat, going through a dancing lesson. They danced to themselves in a mirror, the dance director's voice striking like a metronome. "One, two, three, four and TURN," he said, ". . . and Kevin-Coates-you-turn-on-your-left-foot." Conway absorbed the scene and walked back into his office, lighting another cigarette from the stub of the first. "I'm still limited to the beautiful people," he said. "They've got a Tyrone Power tradition at this Studio and that's what they're looking for." He raised his hands in resignation. "Now Christ, you see someone today who looks like a young Tyrone Power and what's your first reaction? He's got to be some kind of fag. Let's face it, it's hard to identify with the beautiful people. It's the kids who buy the theater tickets, kids from fourteen to twenty-five. And the people the kids identify with are Belmondo, Streisand, McQueen—the people Jack Warner used to call the 'ugs.' They've got the sense of anarchy, right, and that's what the kids like. Streisand, she's an ug. Well, she's an ug who's getting a million bucks from this studio to do *Hello, Dolly!*" He waved his arm in the general direction of the dancing lesson. "You think any of those beautiful people out there are ever going to get a million bucks a picture?" Conway shook his head slowly.

"Someone who's not beautiful isn't conventional," he said. "Out here a beautiful girl is just that—she's got the long hair, the boobs, the nice legs, the suntan. It's more original not to be beautiful. But you try telling the Studio that." He snubbed out his cigarette. "These kids, though, they think they can con me, as long as I've been in the business. There was this one girl, Janine Something, she came in one day for a reading. Wanted to get in the program. Her agent was gushing all over me. Well, she wasn't very good and I gave her the old routine, 'Don't call us, we'll call you.' As it happens, I had to go to the hospital for an operation. I get out of the hospital and her agent calls and I don't return the call. Then one day I get a letter from this Janine. 'Dear Mr. Conway,' it says. 'I'm so glad you're out of the hospital and on the road to recovery. I'm especially glad because I've just had some bad news in my family. My father was in the hospital and they sent him home.' Etc., etc. Cancer of the pancreas, I think it was. Inoperable. And then she says, 'Every night my father looks at me and says, I just want you taken care of, Janine. If you got that Fox contract, I could die happy.' " Conway ran his fingers through his hair. "How do you like them apples?" he said.

The following week, a young actor in the New Talent Program sauntered into the commissary with his new agent, a dark, feral young man scarcely older than his client, very junior in the agency, just a few months out of the mail room. The agent headed for the producers' dining room, but the head waitress steered him to a table in the far corner of the room. Annoyed by his table, the agent started to move back across the commissary, then thought better of it and slipped down next to his client. He snapped an order of cottage cheese and lettuce to the waitress and then bit angrily on a piece of ice.

"We don't take any crap from this studio or any other studio," the agent said. Some of the ice had begun to melt and drip out the corner of his mouth. He berated the waitress for not having a napkin at the table, and when she stared coolly at him, he finally wiped his mouth with the back of his hand. "When you sign with us, we call the shots," he said. "We don't think you should test, you don't test. We don't think you should read, you don't read. They take you on our terms and they don't like it, we take you someplace else."

The young actor spread some butter on a roll. "I like it," he said. "I really like it."

8

It's a superb example of what it is,

George Axelrod said

Early in August the Studio began preparing for a meeting of eighty of its foreign distributors and publicity men from all over the world. The purpose of the gathering was to expose the distributors to the Studio's upcoming pictures that were to be released during the next year. Planning for the convention was left in the hands of the publicity department, which began to resemble an isolated country convent getting ready for the annual visit of the auxiliary bishop. A full schedule of events was evolving. Public Relations had prepared a brochure for the conventioneers with a combination of firm and breezy advice ("You are lodged at the Century Plaza Hotel. No COD's, please, and watch the long distance calls. . . . The hospitality room is Joel Coler's suite on the nineteenth floor, where the advice on all matters is a lot more free-flowing and less reliable than the liquor"). On Stage 2, the actresses and actors in the New Talent School daily rehearsed a variety show prepared especially for the exhibitors; the show consisted of scenes from Fox pictures shooting or in preparation interspersed with patter songs highlighting Studio successes past and present. A trip to Disneyland was on the distributors' itinerary, and arrangements were made for French, German and Spanish-speaking interpreters to guide the delegates over the Matterhorn, through the Jungle Ride and on the Submarine Trip. The final event of the convention was to be a cocktail and dinner party, catered by Chasen's, to be held in the elaborately landscaped garden of director George Cukor. Cukor was just lending his house; he did not plan to attend the party. It was agreed in preliminary discussions to invite only the girls in the New Talent Program to Cukor's; the boys in the Program were scratched unless they had featured billing in a forthcoming Studio production. As a result of a Studio directive, producers of all pictures currently shooting were putting together trailers to show the exhibitors. Darryl Zanuck himself was scheduled to make his first appearance at the Studio since his takeover four years before. A few days before his arrival, posters went up around the lot welcoming the delegates. Each poster showed a waving American flag, a photograph of Darryl Zanuck wearing sunglasses, and the words: "A Salute to the President."

The week before the convention opened, Studio executives from New York and Europe began filtering into Los Angeles. One of the immediate problems facing them was not pictures but parking. Under the terms of its agreement with the Aluminum Company of America, which owns the Century City complex tangent to the Studio, as well as the property on which the Studio stands, Fox has the use of its land under a 99-year lease. In the summer of 1967 there were some 4,000 people working at the Studio, and parking spaces were at a premium. But Alcoa had begun to apply pressure on the Studio to give up some of its parking facilities near the front gate, where Pico Boulevard meets Avenue of the Stars. Alcoa claimed that it wanted to build a high-rise on the Pico lot. But what Alcoa actually desired was a piece of land on the Studio's back lot, near the Century Plaza Hotel, where it wanted to build a hotel garage. The back-lot property was production land, containing both the moat and the tank, where underwater photography and water scenes were shot. Alcoa wanted it because of its accessibility to the Century Plaza. By threatening the Studio with eviction from the Pico lot, Alcoa hoped to persuade Fox to make a deal whereby it offered instead to give up some of its back-lot land. The question before the Studio executives as they filed into Richard Zanuck's office a few days before the convention began was what was more valuable to Fox—the back lot or the Pico parking lot.

"Do we use the moat a lot?" Zanuck said. The Alcoa file was open before him and he cracked his knuckles methodically.

"Five days last year," Stan Hough said.

"How about the green tank?" Zanuck said.

"Thirty days," Hough said.

Zanuck looked surprised. "Even with *Voyage to the Bottom of the Sea?*"

"Yes, Rich, but how little we use it is beside the point," Hough said. As the Studio's production manager, responsible for keeping budgets and below-the-line costs in check, Hough was unalterably opposed to giving up production land. "If you try to rent a tank at another studio for thirty days, you're talking big money."

Zanuck noted Hough's objection with a nod of his head. He brooded for a moment and turned to Harry Sokolov. "Say we give them something in the back lot and they build a garage, do we get any free parking in it?"

"We said we wanted 400 spaces," Sokolov said. "200 free and 200 at a negotiated rate. They won't buy it."

Zanuck began chewing on a fingernail. His eyes blinked rapidly. No one in the room spoke. Finally he picked up a letter from the folder and tapped it with his finger. "Alcoa says they're dealing from strength," he said. "Anybody who puts that kind of statement in a letter is trying to bluff. I say we're the ones dealing from strength."

"Amen," Hough said.

Zanuck acknowledged Hough's interruption with a quick smile. "Let's tell these guys we'll give them 97,000 square feet of the north lot out back and throw in lot four besides. But we'll tell them we want all the Pico lot and won't give up any production land." He looked around the office. "What do you fellows think of that?"

"I'm all for it, Rich," Hough said. He glanced around the room. "I'm speaking from the production angle, of course, but if you start giving up production land, you can't just say we'll build a moat someplace else. You fellows don't realize how much costs have gone up."

There was neither agreement nor disagreement with Hough. Most of the men simply stared into the middle distance, as if weighing the problem. At last Frank Ferguson, the head of the legal department, cleared his throat. "I don't think we should give them an ultimatum, Dick," he said deliberately. "After all, we're going to be neighbors for a long time and they could make things very difficult for us." He looked at the stolid faces around him. "I'd ease up with them, Dick. State your proposition and then say we're prepared to discuss."

"I don't think so, Frank," Zanuck said quickly. "It's not to our advantage to prolong it. Let's smoke them out first—and then we'll discuss."

Arthur Jacobs eased his golf cart into Richard Zanuck's parking place outside the administration building. Mort Abrahams looked at Zanuck's name painted on the curbstone and then back at Jacobs.

"He's gone," Jacobs said. "He's off the lot for a couple of hours."

"How do you know?" Abrahams said doubtfully.

"I know," Jacobs said. "I just know."

He hurried down into the basement toward a screening room. He was running behind schedule. He had a lunch date in Hollywood with Anthony Newley and he had to watch the minifilm of *Planet of the Apes*. Jacobs makes minifilms of all his pictures. They are longer than a trailer, sometimes running thirty-five minutes, spliced together from footage of finished and near-finished pictures, complete with optical effects, montages, whip pans. Jacobs shows each minifilm to exhibitors to stir up enthusiasm before the picture is actually released. He flicked off the lights in the screening room and the minifilm rolled across the screen—the crash of the space ship, the trek of the surviving astronauts across the desert waste, the dawning realization that the evolutionary process had been reversed. Jacobs impatiently made notes throughout the showing, but spoke only once—when Charlton Heston and his fellow space travelers were swimming nude under a waterfall.

"I can see their butts," Jacobs said. "We've got to give the impression of nudity without showing Chuck's ass."

That afternoon, Richard Zanuck watched the previous day's rushes of *Planet of the Apes*. The scene showed an ape doctor giving a blood transfusion. The recipient was Charlton Heston, the donor Linda Harrison, who played Nova, the mute Earth Girl. In angle after angle, the ape fastened the tube between the arms of the two Earth people.

"You don't give a transfusion that way," Owen McLean said in the darkness of the projection room. "You take blood out of one arm first, then pump it into the other arm. You can't make blood flow from arm to arm like that."

"He's right, Dick," Stan Hough said.

Zanuck was unperturbed. "What the hell," he said. "Maybe that's how an ape does it."

David Brown had come out from New York for the exhibitors' convention. The morning after his arrival, he sat in his office, just down the hall from Richard Zanuck's, chewing meditatively on an unlit pipe. A minor crisis had arisen over Frank McCarthy, who was scheduled to produce the roadshow production of *Tom Swift*, with Gene Kelly directing. The same duo had recently teamed on the immensely successful Walter Matthau comedy, *A Guide for the Married Man*. A brigadier general in the U.S. Army Reserve, McCarthy had made for himself a distinguished career in the military and the government before coming to Hollywood. During World War II, he had served as military secretary to General George Marshall, and after the war as an Assistant Secretary of State under James Byrnes. In 1945 he had been selected as one of the U.S. Junior Chamber of Commerce's ten outstanding young men.

The problem concerned *Tom Swift*. Fox scheduled only two roadshow pictures a year, since there were not enough major theaters across the country to handle the number of hard-ticket films the studios had taken to turning out. It was impossible for a studio to make a roadshow picture and then hold it in the can until a theater became available, as the interest rates on the bank loan necessary to finance a film were prohibitive if no theatrical revenues were coming in. Fox had both *Tom Swift* and *Hello, Dolly!* ready to go into production. Though *Hello, Dolly!* was closer to a start date than *Tom Swift*, it had no director set. The *Hello, Dolly!* assignment was a plum. Barbra Streisand had been signed to star, along with Matthau, and the initial budget of $20 million was the largest in Hollywood history. The Studio had finally asked Kelly to direct *Hello, Dolly!*, which meant that *Tom Swift* had to be postponed for at least a year. This left McCarthy with nothing to do. The situation was slightly if obscurely complicated by the fact that McCarthy, as a former winner, had just nominated Richard Zanuck as a Junior Chamber of Commerce "outstanding young man." To assuage McCarthy, Zanuck offered him the producer's spot on a new comedy by writer-director George Axelrod, *The Connecticut Look*. It was a solution that appealed neither to McCarthy nor to Axelrod. Fox's purchase of *The Connecticut Look*, and its assignment of the starring role to Matthau, was in fact partly predicated on the box office returns of McCarthy's *A Guide for the Married Man*. Both were of the Doris Day sex-farce genre—a little slicker, a little gamier (the protagonists actually do make it to bed), but, withal, featuring the same moral uplift at the fadeout: the very married hero of *Guide* takes a crash course in infidelity before deciding in the last reel to keep the home fires burning; in *The Connecticut Look*, a thirtyish housewife turns prostitute for an afternoon's dalliance with an actor to restore her faith in romance, and in the process shores up her shaky marriage. McCarthy was not anxious to produce *The Connecticut Look* nor was Axelrod anxious to have him, and Brown had been assigned by Zanuck to resolve the problem diplomatically.

Brown tapped his pipe on an ashtray and buzzed Zanuck's office. "Dick, I talked to Frank about Axelrod," he said. "He said he'd do it if you wanted him to, he's got nothing but the highest respect for you, but he has reservations. He's worried about the morals of George's picture. He's afraid the guy and the girl will die a lingering death and he doesn't want to do anything that will reflect on the success of *Guide*."

Brown listened for a moment. "Yes, Dick, I told George that Frank had the highest personal regard for him and that he knew that George would direct this picture with the greatest of taste. But Frank's worried about what this story will do to him. 'I'm worried about me,' is the way he put it. You understand, his being a general and all, and a good personal friend of Omar Bradley's. He doesn't want to make a film that will expose him to personal criticism. I think I understand his predicament, Dick. Let me talk to George and I'm sure we can iron something out."

George Axelrod came into Brown's office later that morning, a tall, nervous man in his mid-forties wearing chino pants, a windbreaker and black velvet pumps on which his initials were stitched in gold. He had written the enormously successful Broadway play, *The Seven-Year Itch*, two other Broadway hits, a number of screenplays (including *The Manchurian Candidate*, which he considered one of the two great films ever made in Hollywood, the other being *Citizen Kane*), and directed one previous picture. Puffing fiercely on a cigarette, he paced back and forth across Brown's office.

"I've known Frank for years," Axelrod said. "Socially and professionally, and I've got nothing but the highest personal regard for him. In a given circumstance, he would be marvelous as a producer, just great." He stabbed the air with his cigarette. "However—and here it is—I saw *Guide for the Married Man*. It's a *superb* example of what it is. But it's a different picture. It's not my picture." Axelrod stopped and picked up an ashtray. "I don't want to destroy my . . ." he sought the proper word ". . . my *thrust*. I'm amenable to any Fox guy you put on the picture, but I just don't want to destroy my thrust. And of course I assure you I'm going to do this picture with *impeccable* taste."

"I know that, George," Brown said placidly. "We're just worried about the specter of *Kiss Me, Stupid*."

Axelrod interrupted his pacing and threw up his hands. "I'm not going to be put in the *preposterous* position of saying anything against Billy Wilder, who is the greatest filmmaker in the world."

"Taste is the thing," Brown said.

"Look, I'm not going to make a picture you can't release," Axelrod said.

"I know that, George."

"My fear is having someone in a high position on this picture who is not sympathetic to my views," Axelrod said. He stalked the room, picking up and putting down ashtrays. "But I don't want to be placed in a position where I offend Frank, who is a friend."

"I know," Brown said.

Axelrod changed his tack. "You know, the late Judy Holliday had the kind of *purity* the girl in this part needs."

"She would have been wonderful," Brown said. He had not shifted position in his chair.

"And I think the scene with the girl and the movie star in the bedroom is the best thing I've ever written," Axelrod said.

"He comes off very sympathetic in the end," Brown said.

"That's right," Axelrod said.

"And he started off as such a shit," Brown said.

"That's the beauty of the scene," Axelrod said.

Brown's pipe had gone out and he leaned forward and refilled it. "Look," he said. "We'll talk to Frank and see if we can reconcile our differences. And if we can't, we'll get a guy on the picture who can function as a high-level assistant."

Axelrod inhaled deeply and shook his head slowly from side to side as he blew the smoke out. "Just someone who can get Doc Merman off my back when he says we can't afford a $75-a-week second-assistant assistant."

"There's a lot of guys on the lot like that," Brown said. "We can give them a credit of associate producer or something like that."

"That would be perfect, David," Axelrod said.

Frank McCarthy did not produce *The Connecticut Look*. The picture was retitled *The Secret Life of an American Wife* and was produced, as well as written and directed, by George Axelrod.

The weather was still gray and gloomy at the beach where *The Sweet Ride* was shooting. Joe Pasternak came out of the beach house and examined the sky. "There's nothing for the producer to do," he said. "I come out, I check, I pat everyone on the back, I say what went wrong, but there's nothing I can do." The sun was trying to burn away the overcast. "Except pray the sun doesn't come out. The sun comes out now, the whole day is ruined."

On the sundeck of the house, *The Sweet Ride*'s director, Harvey Hart, was setting up a shot over the shoulders of the picture's stars, Michael Sarrazin and Jacqueline Bisset, down to the beach, where the scene called for them to watch the approach of Hell's Angels-type motorcyclists. Sarrazin fished out a cigarette and lit it.

"Is that a cork tip?" the script girl said.

Sarrazin nodded.

"You were smoking a white filter in the last shot," the script girl said.

Hart produced a white filter cigarette and gave it to Sarrazin. Hart shouted down to the beach for someone to make a mark where the motorcyclists were to stop so that they could remain in the shot.

"That's the toughest thing for an actor to learn," Pasternak said. "Hitting the mark. A young actor starts looking for the mark, then the shot's no good. The old pros hit the mark without even looking."

Jacqueline Bisset took her place at the railing of the sundeck. The camera was behind her, looking down over her at the figures on the beach.

Pasternak shook his head sadly. "How can you tell a director that this shot isn't worth shooting?" he said. "He should do a reverse and show her standing on the porch. You get her face that way." He started back up the steps for his car. "And I'm selling a face, not an ass."

When he got back to the Studio, Pasternak immediately went into a screening room to watch the previous day's rushes of *The Sweet Ride*. It was a scene, shot from a number of different angles, in which Tony Franciosa and Jacqueline discuss her relationship with

Sarrazin. After the lights came on in the projection room, Pasternak sat for a long time in his chair, his hands folded in his lap.

"There's no closeup of Tony," Pasternak said at last.

"I told Harvey that," *The Sweet Ride*'s film editor said. "He said he didn't want one."

Pasternak's pale blue eyes darted around the screening room. "This guy's in love with long shots," he said. "What's he got against faces?"

Back in his office, Pasternak told his secretary to call Richard Day, the art director who had done the sets for *The Sweet Ride*. "Dick," he said, when Day was finally located, "do we have any stills on the beach house?" He listened for a moment. "Well, I want you to send a photographer down there and shoot it from every angle. Just like it is now. Once we leave, we can't go back, and I need the stills in case we have to build a set of the house back here at the Studio." His hands were shaking slightly. "Just to get some closeups."

Two days later, Pasternak stood in the hot summer sun outside the Studio administration building talking to Tom Mankiewicz, who had written the screenplay of *The Sweet Ride* and who was the young son of director Joseph Mankiewicz.

"I've been working on the trailer for the convention," Pasternak said.

"How long is it?" Mankiewicz said.

"Ten minutes," Pasternak said. "But it's not how long it is, it's how it sticks out. The opening shot is Jackie Bisset coming out of the water with no clothes on. Those guys have got to like that."

9

For when we show it in Israel,

Harry Sokolov said

The exhibitors' convention officially opened the second Monday in August. The end of the previous week, Darryl Zanuck had arrived at the Studio with a minimum of fanfare and had not accompanied the delegates on their Sunday junket to Disneyland. The highlight of the opening day's activities was a sneak preview at the Village Theater in Westwood of the Studio's latest Frank Sinatra picture, *Tony Rome*, the story of a sleazy Miami private detective "up to his neck," as a Studio publicist put it, "in booze, broads, blackmail and bodies." The distributors had arrived at the theater in buses and been herded inside by teams of public relations men, past a crowd of gawking onlookers. Parked by the curb outside the theater was a fleet of Cadillac limousines for the Studio executives. The preview was virtually a command performance for all the major producers on the lot, and when the picture was over, the delegates congregated in little groups around various Studio producers and executives outside the theater. Harry Sokolov was in an exuberant mood.

"It's a good product," Sokolov said. His physique resembles three balloons set one atop the other. "I like all of our product. You know why? It's diversified. We've got something for everybody."

There was a general murmur of agreement.

"Something for everybody," said Abe Dickstein, the balding domestic sales manager who had come out from New York for the meeting. "A nice picture like *Two for the Road*, you got Audrey Hepburn, you'll win some awards, you give it special attention, you'll turn a little profit. It's nice, sure, but you take a *Tony Rome*, a *Valley of the Dolls*, now those are the pictures you like to sell."

One of the European delegates asked the cost of *Tony Rome*, and when told, he mused that *Alfie*, *Georgie Girl*, *Morgan* and *Blow-up* combined had not cost so much, and all were enormously successful. As if talking to himself, he wondered if it weren't sometimes better to make a small picture and hope for a large return.

"Sure, *Alfie* was successful," said James Denton, the head of the Studio's West Coast publicity department. He is a large benign man with a mane of white hair. "But think what it could have done if it had stars. Jack Lemmon, for instance, and Shirley MacLaine."

The morning after the *Tony Rome* sneak, Richard Zanuck sat yawning prodigiously in his office. It had been a late night. After the preview, Frank Sinatra had hosted a party for the exhibitors at the Century Plaza, and when that broke up, Sinatra and the two Zanucks had adjourned to The Daisy, a private discothèque in Beverly Hills. The evening had not ended until after three o'clock, but Richard Zanuck was at his office promptly at 8:30 for his daily staff meeting with Stan Hough, Harry Sokolov, Owen McLean and David Brown, who always attends when he is in from New York. The evening had taken its toll and everyone sat around reading the trade papers. In the bar off Zanuck's office, Brown was on the telephone to his story department in New York, which had called him about a novel then being offered to all the film companies.

"What are they asking?" Brown said. *"Three hundred thousand."* He repeated the figure over again slowly. "Well, I've read it and thought it was terrible, but for that kind of money, I guess we should show it to Dick."

Brown hung up the phone and came back into the main office. "DZ go the distance last night?" he asked.

"Oh, yeah," Zanuck said. A hesitant smile creased his tanned face. "Oh, yeah." He yawned and leaned back in his chair. "I didn't think the screening went too well," he said.

"You got to figure it's a blasé audience in Westwood," Hough said. No one else looked up from the trades. "Everyone there knows how to make a movie better than we do." He shrugged. "I thought it was just a bit under the Fresno sneak."

"I was talking to the guy from Israel and he said we'd

have to change a lot of the dialogue," Harry Sokolov said. "For when we show it in Israel."

"It will go right over their head, the slang," Hough said.

"There won't be any problem," Zanuck said. "We'll just dub it in the local slang."

"What do they speak there?" Hough said. "Yiddish?"

"I don't know," Sokolov said. "Hebrew maybe."

"A little German," Brown said.

"Shi-i-i-t," Hough said.

"What's pussy in Hebrew, Harry?" Owen McLean said. There was a scene in the picture based on the *double-entendre* of an old woman calling her cat a "pussy."

"You guys are always putting me on," Sokolov said. "How the hell am I supposed to know? Just because I'm Jewish?"

Zanuck closed up the trades. "We're going to get Nancy Sinatra to sing the title song over the credits of *Tony Rome*," he said. "I haven't heard it yet, but that's a promotable parlay, Nancy singing the title song over Frank's picture."

Later that morning, Harry McIntyre dropped into Richard Zanuck's office. McIntyre was the secretary of the Twentieth Century Fox Film Corporation and, like the other officers of the company, was in Los Angeles for the convention. The Studio was considering financing and distributing foreign films, and McIntyre, a harried financial executive with a tremulous, whiny voice, was bearish on the prospect.

"It's okay with the French and Italian pictures, Dick,"

he said. "A lot of those people, you know their track record. You take a Fellini, a Truffaut, you know what those fellows can do. It's the other countries I'm afraid of. You take this picture *Dr. Glas.* Jesus, I never heard of it. I mean, who do you know makes pictures in Yugoslavia? I'm not saying they're not good, but you got to consider the track record, it seems to me, Dick."

Zanuck nodded. "In France and Italy, you know the talent."

"Dick, I got the track record from the past," McIntyre said. "You take a lot of those countries over there and it's like dropping money down a well." He shuddered. "*Czechoslovakia.*" His voice became more tremulous. "There's another thing that scares me. You can't have control. And then you're talking about revolving credit."

"If there's anything that scares me, it's a revolving fund," Zanuck said. "You make a profit on the first one, but then the damn thing's gone, revolving into some other goddamn place."

"That's right, Dick," McIntyre said. "And you've got to look at the track record. Remember *La Fuga.*" His shoulders shook again. "My God."

Peter Glenville filmed his three-hour version of Graham Greene's The Comedians *with an intermission, but the break will be used only in Europe where the movie is to be shown on a reserved seat basis. There'll be a "continuous performance" policy in the United States, Glenville says, because the picture could lose its topicality if the Haitian regime it treats were suddenly overthrown: "Haiti is one hour and 20 minutes away from Miami."*

Joyce Haber, The Los Angeles Times

The day before the convention ended, Arthur Jacobs booked a private dining room in the commissary for a luncheon with a half dozen of the Studio's foreign publicity supervisors from France, England, Scandinavia, Australia, the Far East and Latin America. The purpose of the lunch was to coordinate the foreign promotional and publicity campaigns for *Dr. Dolittle*. It was a brutally hot day, and although the air conditioner was working at top speed, the heat in the dining room was oppressive. Jacobs sat halfway down one side of the large table fanning himself with a napkin. "Have the melon," he kept on saying, "it's the only thing on a day like this."

"Is the cantaloupe ripe?" asked Bernard Flatow, the Latin American representative.

"Who cares if it's ripe?" Jacobs said. "A day like this, what are you going to order, Salisbury steak and au gratin potatoes?"

Most of the men took off their jackets and hung them over the backs of their chairs. Flatow picked at his melon and suggested an international teaser campaign conducted in the personal columns of papers throughout Latin America. He wore thick glasses and had a thin mustache. "You put in something funny like, 'Elephant seeks partner in trunk business, contact Dr. Dolittle,' something funny and cute like that, the response you get will be tremendous," Flatow said. "Anyone who answers will get a circular about the picture." He looked at Jacobs. "What do you think of that, Arthur? It's a real cute idea."

Jacobs lit a cigarettello and canvassed the table with his eyes. The other men looked at him blankly. "Send me a memo on it," he said finally.

The table was cleared and the delegates hunched over their coffee. All the foreign representatives wanted a major star from *Dr. Dolittle* present when the picture premiered in their areas, and it was a question of who would get whom. Rex Harrison was definitely scheduled for the Paris, London, New York and Los Angeles openings, and there was a possibility that he would also go to Tokyo.

"We can't count on anything more than that at this time," Jacobs said. "I just don't think we can get any further commitments out of Rex until after the New York reviews come out."

"They're going to be brilliant, Arthur," one of the delegates said.

"Well, that's what we're hoping," Jacobs said. "But if they're not, he's not going to be embarrassed. You know Rex. You can't push him." He shoved aside a coffee cup and spread out a list of all the foreign openings. The problem now was to allot the other three stars of the picture—Samantha Eggar, Anthony Newley and Richard Attenborough—to the various premieres.

"Does Newley mean anything in Japan?" Jacobs said.

"Not a thing," the Far Eastern representative said.

"How about Australia?" Jacobs said.

"He'll be very big there," the Australian delegate said.

"He's got a lot of other commitments, but we'll try to pencil him in for Australia," Jacobs said. "Who wants Attenborough?"

"He's definite for New York, London and Los Angeles," Mort Abrahams said.

Jacobs puffed on his thin black cigarette. "I'd rather he went to Toronto than come out here," he said.

"That's the twenty-second of December, the night after we open in Los Angeles. We don't have anyone for Toronto, and it's important we get someone there. I mean, they don't expect Rex in places like that, but they would like someone, and Dickie would be great."

"He's got his heart set on coming to Los Angeles," Abrahams said. "And he can't go to both."

Jacobs blinked rapidly. "Let me call him," he said. He went to the telephone by the window and placed a person-to-person call to Attenborough in England. It was several moments before the overseas operator was able to complete the call. Jacobs checked his watch. "It'll be eleven o'clock there, right?" he said. No one paid any attention. Finally the call got through. "Dickie? Arthur." Jacobs' voice was too loud, as if it were a bad connection. He and Attenborough exchanged small talk about Attenborough's wife, his children, how the picture looked and what the weather was like in England before getting to the point. "Look, Dickie," Jacobs said, "how'd you like to go to the premiere in Toronto? Great, I thought you would. But look, Dickie, there's one small hitch. Toronto's the night after Los Angeles and I don't think you can make both." Jacobs listened and looked around the table. "You say Sheila has her heart set on coming to Los Angeles? She likes the smog, huh? Yeah, it's smoggier than hell in December. The thing is, Dickie, the whole premiere in Toronto will be built around you, they're really anxious to have you, I didn't know you were that big in Canada. . . . Sure, Dickie, I understand, you've got a lot of friends here. Well, we're dying to see you, too, Dickie. But think Toronto and send me a cable, okay?"

Jacobs replaced the phone and made a rolling and pitching motion with his hand to indicate that it was still up in the air about Attenborough's going to Canada.

"Let's talk about Latin America," Flatow said. "We've got to do something about Latin America."

"Who?" Jacobs said. He still seemed preoccupied with Attenborough and the northern part of the hemisphere.

"Well, as you know, the pushmi-pullyus for the lobby displays are being made in Peru," Flatow said. The pushmi-pullyu, a mythical, two-headed llama in the script, was one of the major motifs in the Studio's advertising campaign for *Dr. Dolittle*. "I'd like to hold a lot of press interviews and say how these lobby displays really help Peruvian cottage industry, and it would really help if we can get Harrison down for the Lima opening."

"Not a chance," Abrahams said.

"What if I can get him decorated by the Peruvian government?" Flatow said. "I think I can get him, I don't know . . . the Condor of the Andes, or something like that."

"What for?" Abrahams asked incredulously.

"Like I just said," Flatow replied. "For helping Peruvian cottage industry."

"Condor of the Andes first class or second class?" Jacobs said. "You know Rex, he loves decorations."

"I can only get it if he shows up in Lima," Flatow said. "If not, forget it. But if you can get a commitment out of him, Arthur, I can start turning the screws on the Peruvian government."

"I'll talk to him," Jacobs said.

To further the publicity campaign for *Dr. Dolittle*, Rex Harrison, at the request of Arthur Jacobs, compiled a list of quotes he had made about his wife, the actress Rachel Roberts. "Dear Arthur," Harrison's memorandum to Jacobs read:

> Here are some of the things I have said about Rachel. I can find you lots more if you want.
> "Rachel is a joy to me—she has the unusual blend of sense and nonsense, which I find irresistible. She is capable of great love and violent emotion like all true Celts.
> "She has a wonderful brain, which she manages to disguise behind an amused exterior.
> "She is a truly fine actress and I find that comforting, as her advice to me is always unfailingly right."
> Rex

The New Talent Program's show for the exhibitors was held on Stage 15 the night before the convention ended. The students performed scenes from *Justine, Hello, Dolly!, The Sweet Ride, Valley of the Dolls* and a number of other Studio pictures. The show was well received by the exhibitors, although some of the producers winced visibly at the interpretation given their films by the neophyte actors and actresses. After the performance, the Studio held a barbecue on the Western street, a permanent set of a town in the Old West, where the guests were serenaded by a country orchestra and a U.S. Marine Corps band. At the barbecue, it was generally agreed that the New Talent School was a wonderful idea and that the students were terribly talented.

Darryl and Richard Zanuck attended the New Talent

School show, but slipped out before the barbecue on the Western street. With David Brown, the two Zanucks dined instead at The Bistro, perhaps the most fashionable restaurant in Beverly Hills. Richard Zanuck was accompanied by Linda Harrison, and Darryl Zanuck by a willowy French girl named Genevieve. The Bistro is owned jointly by some sixty stockholders, most of whom have a stake in the picture business and who include such impeccable Industry names as Billy Wilder and Frank Sinatra. The maître d' and one of the stockholders is a tall stern-looking German named Kurt Niklas, who has a highly developed sense of the local pecking order, and the walls of the restaurant are lined with antiqued mirrors so that it is possible from any table to see anyone else in the restaurant without an undue show of inquisitiveness. The favored small table is in the corner, under the stairs; the favored table for parties of six or more, right next to it on the north wall. It was to this table that the Zanuck party was led. There is an almost studied indifference at The Bistro to Industry personalities, but practically every head in the room swiveled as the Zanucks took their places. They ordered dinner oblivious to the stares directed at them, talking all the time of the Studio and its various projects. Linda Harrison listened with rapt attention, nodding her head at every point, while Darryl Zanuck's companion, who spoke little English, fiddled with a cigar, waiting for someone to light it. When no one did, she lit it herself. As the dinner wore on, the conversation switched to the Zanucks' various athletic accomplishments. Puffing on a cigar, the candlelight glinting off his sunglasses, Darryl Zanuck reminisced about his polo-playing days.

"Dad," Richard Zanuck interrupted, "Dad . . ."

"We played a tough game in those days," Darryl Zanuck said.

"Dad, Jesus, Dad," Richard Zanuck said. "I'll say it was tough. You remember that day, I was just a kid, I came into the bathroom upstairs and you were bent over bleeding into the tub. Jesus, it was like a slaughterhouse."

"Bleeding," Darryl Zanuck said. "I should have been bleeding. I got a mallet in the face."

"I bet you finished the game, though, Darryl," David Brown said.

The elder Zanuck chewed on his cigar. Other sports were discussed and then Richard Zanuck's days as a prep school football player at the Harvard Military Academy in Los Angeles.

"I remember one game," Richard Zanuck said. "It was against Compton. I wasn't captain. We took a bus down there and they were the biggest bunch of guys I ever saw. A lot of big colored guys." He poured some red wine. "I don't think we had anyone as big as their smallest guy."

"I remember that game," Darryl Zanuck said from across the table. His companion assumed an interested look. "I went down to watch it. I was sitting next to this guy and he said, 'The only guys with any guts on that team are my son and that Zanuck kid.'"

David Brown raised his glass. "I'll drink to that," he said.

The following night, the convention came to an end with the cocktail and dinner party at director George Cukor's home in the Hollywood Hills. Cukor greeted the delegates and then quietly disappeared. White balloons floated in the swimming pool and an orchestra played the score of *Dr. Dolittle*. Arthur Jacobs stood at the edge of the pool with Natalie Trundy, an intermittent actress who was also Jacobs' intermittent fiancée, discussing the picture's upcoming sneak preview in Minneapolis.

"I'm not nervous," Jacobs said.

"Oh, no, you're not nervous," Natalie Trundy said. "Not *very* nervous."

"Fleischer's nervous," Jacobs said. "I'm not nervous. It's only a preview."

"All I know," Natalie Trundy said, "is that when we go to Minneapolis, I'm going to take along a big bottle of Miltown and slip it all into that vodka you drink so much of."

Jacobs stepped back and studied the balloons floating in the pool. "Fleischer's nervous as hell," he said.

10
" *Hello, Mother,* **"**

Paul Monash said

The week after the convention, Richard Zanuck left for Europe both to take a vacation in the South of France and to meet with executives on Studio pictures shooting in England and on the Continent. He was not scheduled to return to the United States until the first sneak preview of *Dr. Dolittle* in Minneapolis the second week of September. In his absence, business at the Studio functioned as usual. With Gene Kelly set as director, *Hello, Dolly!* began to take shape. The Studio had bought the musical two and a half years before for $2,100,000 and had signed Ernest Lehman both to produce and to direct. Based on the cost of other musicals, Zanuck estimated that *Hello, Dolly!* would cost between $12 million and $15 million, but the preliminary estimate based on Lehman's first-draft screenplay placed the budget at $25 million.

Immediately the Studio went to work to pare the budget back within reason. Department by department, item by item, costs were questioned; the number of extras was cut, the number of horses used in street scenes was cut, shooting days were cut, streets and buildings used in the exterior set of New York City were cut. Still the budget was too high. The biggest item was the exterior set of New York. It was originally planned to build the New York set at the Fox ranch in Malibu, but after months of surveys on costs and the arc of the sun (where would the sun be during the prime shooting hours if the set were constructed on a north-south axis? on an east-west axis?), the Malibu site was abandoned. In the first place, there was no way that the set could be constructed without the Santa Monica Mountains forming a backdrop for the New York skyline. Secondly, the cost of trucking building materials out to Malibu, on top of the already staggering construction estimates, would have made the set budget prohibitive. And lastly, there were the unions. Under union rules, crew members must report to the Studio proper before proceeding, by Studio vehicles, to the scene of location shooting. Though the ranch was owned by the Studio, it was an hour's drive from the Westwood lot and by definition, under the various union contracts, a "location." Thus, if the New York sets were built at the ranch, two hours a day would be lost driving to and from Malibu; this meant that it would take four days of Malibu shooting to accomplish what could be done in three elsewhere.

The question was where. The first panicky sugges-

tions were to shoot *Hello, Dolly!* in Europe, either in
Spain or in Rome. Indeed a budget was drawn up on
the basis of Roman shooting that showed a minimum
saving of several million dollars. But the idea of European locations was emphatically vetoed by Zanuck.
"Jesus, you can get away with shooting *Cleopatra* in
Rome," he told me one day, "but *Hello, Dolly!* is a
piece of hard-core Americana. You shoot that in Rome
and the unions back here will raise such a stink you'll
have a hard time getting over it. It would have tar-
nished the image of the whole picture." Other suggestions were met with equal resistance. Lehman visited
a number of back lots at other studios, and at one
time was even considering the burned-out Atlanta
railroad station from *Gone with the Wind* that still
stood on the Desilu lot. But Fox was reluctant to spend
so much money and then leave a set standing at another studio. Almost in desperation, the Studio decided to make do with the streets and parking lots of
its main lot in Westwood.

The problem was finding enough room. The set designed by *Hello, Dolly!*'s production designer, John De-
Cuir, was physically huge. It involved a complex of sixty
buildings reproduced to resemble Manhattan's Mulberry
Street, Broadway and Fifth Avenue. The total area required was fifteen acres. Through part of the set ran a
600-foot re-creation of the Sixth Avenue el, complete
with a working steam engine and three cars. In some
places, the buildings were to rise to a height of 130 feet,
or eleven stories. They were to be supported by 120 pine
telephone poles and nearly nine miles of steel tubing.
Because of the stresses of the wind against the fragile

mini-skyscrapers, it was necessary to embed all the supporting materials eight feet deep in concrete. Streets had to be paved with simulated granite blocks resembling those used in the period. It was an enormous undertaking and every available foot of Studio space was used. The guest parking lot in front of the administration building was closed. The facing of the sound stages and even that of the administration building were transformed into lower Manhattan. Service roads were torn up and repaved to simulate the Gay 90's. The one set, which would be struck at the completion of *Hello, Dolly!*, cost $1.6 million.

While *Hello, Dolly!* was being readied for production, *Dr. Dolittle* was in the final stages of scoring and mixing prior to the Minneapolis sneak preview. The picture, as befitted its $18 million budget, was scheduled to be the Studio's major contender in the Academy Award race, and both Arthur Jacobs and the publicity department were deep in plans and campaigns to promote the film. A few days after the convention, Jacobs prepared an agenda of items he was to discuss in New York with Jonas Rosenfield, the vice president in charge of advertising and promotion, and other Manhattan-based Studio executives. One section of the agenda was titled

SPECIAL EXPLOITATION
(To Be Discussed at New York Meetings)
    1. APJ and Jack Hirschberg [an Apjac press agent] are currently investigating the cost of a personalized simulated leather album to be called "The Dr. Dolittle Musical Omnibus" and to contain the 20th Century Fox

sound track album, the Reprise Sammy Davis album, the Atlantic Bobby Darin album, the EMI instrumental album, and several of the more important singles, such as Tony Bennett, Andy Williams, Pet Clark.

This would be a deluxe gift for key personnel both here and abroad and would have their names embossed on the album. We are currently getting costs from Jonas Rosenfield.

2. JUNGLELAND: A permanent display at Jungleland of the DOLITTLE compound is being finalized by Jack Hirschberg. All Jungleland trucks will have DOCTOR DO-LITTLE painted on them.

3. "FABULOUS PLACES": It has been suggested that the song "FABULOUS PLACES" can be made very valuable in conjunction with airlines and travel agencies. Last week at the Convention, it was agreed that the various foreign representatives will contact their domestic airlines to ascertain how far this could go in regard to:

    a. playing our sound track on the actual planes

    b. playing the tape at airports, etc.

If the plans are fulfilled for Tony Newley to film "FAB-ULOUS PLACES" at the Los Angeles Airport, this piece of film might well be used for travel agencies as well as airlines. APJ will personally discuss this with TWA next week, as well as the idea of having a special DOLITTLE plane from TWA to cover the premieres in conjunction with JAL.

The foreign representatives were also going to see if the various airlines will use the DOLITTLE brochures in the seat pockets on each flight. It is now available in English, French and Spanish.

4. Vincent LaBella of the Fox Rome office is having samples of Pushmi-Pullyu cuff links and tie clasps made. Mass distribution of this should be explored.

5. DISCUSS: Local Boards of Education to declare DOCTOR DOLITTLE DAY and release children from school.

6. DISCUSS: Award from the Society for the Prevention of Cruelty to Animals.

7. DISCUSS: Award from the American Humane Association.
8. Explore DOLITTLE figure in Madame Tussaud's
Waxworks in both London and Los Angeles.
9. Explore special citation from Congressional Record.
10. Discuss Vatican screening.

As the end of the summer approached, the Studio's
television arm was working at top speed getting ready
for the fall season. Fox had more shows and more pro-
gramming hours than any other studio. One of its new
shows was an hour-long Western called *Custer*. The
title part in the series had been assigned to an unknown
young actor named Wayne Maunder. Maunder's contract was an exclusive seven-year pact and called for an
initial salary of $250 a week, with a $500 bonus for
every segment of the series in which he appeared. The
initial word-of-mouth on the series was that it was a hit
(the new season was supposed to start another Western
cycle on TV) and Maunder's agents, the Ashley-Famous
Artists Agency, were beginning to get restive at the
terms of his contract. So that the series could get into
production, Maunder had signed what is known as a
"short-form contract," which is in essence a letter of
agreement that functions legally until a standard contract, with all its clauses and provisos, can be prepared.
Late one afternoon in the latter part of August, two
AFA agents, Ed Rothman and Robert Wald, walked into
Owen McLean's office. Their mission was to pry better
terms for Maunder out of the Studio before letting him
sign the long-form contract. With McLean were Jack
Baur and two Studio attorneys, both with copies of
Maunder's short-form contract on their laps.

A short young man with a strained and husky voice, Rothman sat down on the couch, pulled out a pen and balanced a yellow legal pad on his knee. McLean leaned back in his desk chair, a set negotiating smile on his face. He and Rothman exchanged pleasantries about the difficulty of finding parking spaces on the Studio lot since the beginning of construction on the *Hello, Dolly!* set. "Well," McLean said finally.

Rothman, who was also an attorney, sighed. "Well, going in we didn't have a lot of bargaining power," he said.

"What makes you think you have now?" McLean said.

"You know what the standard Fox contract is called in the trade?" Rothman said, fencing. "A slave contract."

McLean examined his fingernails, smiling benignly. "I don't recall you calling it that before the boy was signed," he said. "And you seem to have forgotten that we exercised our option before the series was even sold. So I don't think it's exactly a slave contract."

"But he's the star of a series now," Rothman persisted. "There are all kinds of ancillary rights when you're the star of a series, and you're not giving them to him."

"Ed, explain ancillary rights," Baur said.

"Come on, Jack, you know what I mean," Rothman said. "The series is a hit, he'll get invited on all the variety shows. I mean, do you have the right to put him on the Dean Martin show, say, for $250, charge Martin $7,500 and pocket the difference?"

"We sure do," McLean said.

"Well, we think there ought to be a bonus clause for things like radio and television guest appearances," Rothman said.

McLean placed his elbows on his desk and sucked his lips tight against his teeth. "Ed," he said patiently, "let's not try to renegotiate this contract now. Look, the boy was happy when we brought him out here and happy as hell when we picked up his option. And don't forget, we paid his dental bill—which we didn't have to do."

"I was told you didn't," Rothman said. "I was told you loaned him the money for the dental work and took it out of his salary."

"You were told wrong," McLean said equably. He was obviously enjoying the session. "We paid $2,000 for the dental work. Out of *our* pocket. His mouth was in such lousy shape he probably couldn't even get out of bed by now. Every tooth in his head was infected, his gums, everything." He shook his head distastefully. "And this happened even before he came to Fox."

Rothman raised his hand. "All right, all right, I'm overwhelmed by your charity. It's not unusual for a studio to try to keep everything and it's not unusual for a good agent to try and loosen up the contract a little."

McLean smiled. "No chance."

Rothman perused his notes. "What about loanouts?" he said. "We want him to have a piece of what you get if you loan him out to Metro, say, for a picture."

"Negative," Baur said. "It's inherent in all our term contracts that we can loan an actor out anywhere we want."

"We haven't asked the boy to guide any tours yet,"

McLean said. The proceedings seemed to amuse him vastly.

"We have an exclusive deal," Baur said. "If we want to send him down to the beach to ride a surfboard, we can do it."

"And he doesn't get anything, I suppose," Rothman said.

"Correct," Baur said.

"Look, Ed," McLean said, "have you ever heard of a Fox contract where a guy participated in loanouts?"

Rothman shrugged sadly. "I can't recall," he said.

"And you won't," McLean said. "And you know and we know you wouldn't be in here if this series hadn't sold, right?"

Rothman nodded his head back and forth. For a moment, no one spoke. Then Rothman seemed to catch his second wind. He said that as *Custer* was a Western, Maunder would very probably be inundated with rodeo offers on weekends and when the show was not shooting. A rodeo appearance meant merely that Maunder would ride around the arena in costume, but many rodeos offered television stars up to $5,000 a day just for showing up. Rothman contended that a clause should be written into the contract guaranteeing Maunder any rodeo earnings.

McLean shook his head. "The first time someone offers this boy $5,000 a day for a rodeo, you're going to come in here bitching like hell trying to renegotiate this contract." He sucked on his glasses and smiled again. "It hasn't happened yet, so let's save something for then —if he gets it."

Rothman hunched his shoulders and folded up his

notes. "You guys are tough people to deal with," he said.

McLean shook his hand. "You'll be back," he said. "I can count on it."

When Rothman and Wald were gone, McLean put his feet on the edge of his desk. "They were just fishing," he said. "It's a rule of nature. You put an unknown in a series, you sell the series, automatically his agents are going to be in here trying to get a new deal, they want this, they want that. If we start giving them all those things, we've got no place to go, we've got no leverage. Say we gave this boy the bonus, the rodeos. Then if he started getting difficult, he won't do this, he won't do that, he won't make this appearance, he won't do that picture, we've got nothing to lean on him with. Look, we'll let him do a rodeo or a guest shot if it doesn't conflict with his schedule, we'll let him do it and let him keep the money." He tapped his chest. "But out of the goodness of our heart. We won't write it in any contract. You do that, you lose your leverage."

A few days later, Maunder signed the long-form contract. The terms were as stipulated in the short form—$250 a week initial salary with a $500 bonus for every show in which he appeared. He would receive no contractual remuneration for such ancillary rights as rodeos or radio and television guest appearances. His salary would be raised every option period. "It really doesn't mean that much," McLean said. "If the show's a hit, the contract will have to be renegotiated. There's just too many ways the star of a series has you over a barrel. He can claim he's sick and not show up, he can show up late, he can make trouble on the set. What are you going to do? You build a series around a star. He's not there, you don't have a show. A series is bang, bang, into the can, start the next segment. There's not any time for temperament. So when the star gets balky and his agents come to see you, you renegotiate and try and get the best deal you can."

"Most TV shows are what I call Donna Reed's living room," Irwin Allen said during a break in the shooting on Stage 18. "Donna goes to the door, opens the door and there's the milkman. 'Oh, hello, John,' she says. 'Two light cream, three heavy cream.' But John's got a problem, so they go into the living room, sit on the couch and talk for seven pages. 'Oh, John, you found out your wife is giving you a surprise birthday party and you don't want her to know you know.' They shoot the seven pages and then they go home for the day. Me, if I can't blow up the world in the first ten seconds, then the show is a flop."

Allen was not blowing up the world in the show he was preparing, but in the first moments of the initial segment of the series, he was planning to crash a space ship on an uncharted planet populated by giants. The name of the series was *Land of the Giants*; it was created by Allen and, as with all his projects, he was directing the first episode. The show was scheduled as a midseason replacement on the ABC Television Network in the event that any of its fall entries faltered in the ratings; if there was no need for a replacement, *Land of the Giants* would go on the air the following fall.

Allen drank some orange juice and patted his stomach, producing a loud belch. On the adjoining stage, his crew was setting up the crash shot. The passengers on the space ship included the pilot and co-pilot (who was a Negro), a stewardess, an orphan, an international con man with a bagful of swag from his latest caper, a Howard Hughes-type businessman, and a girl described in the script as a "socialite-swinger." On the strange planet, they would be in effect Lilliputians; all the props were built on a scale of twelve-to-one—tree trunks were thirty feet in diameter, safety pins four feet long, tables thirty-six feet high.

The shot was finally ready, and Allen, still drinking orange juice, checked the camera. A cutout of the spacecraft's cockpit was canted on a platform that the crew would roll forward through the giant-sized prop underbrush, simulating the crash landing. Allen's camera was placed to the rear of the platform and would photograph the crash over the space ship's control panel and out the cockpit window. Allen was in good humor and began feeling the muscles of the crew members who would push the platform.

"Okay, fellows," he said. "When I say go, shake, rock, roll and return. This is jiffy productions, instant crashes of ultramodern space ships." He yelled for some fog and a prop man laid a coverlet of artificial fog over the set.

"Action," Allen shouted. "Shake. Rock. Roll. Return." The crew pushed the platform, their muscles straining. The spacecraft scuttled through the underbrush and the fog. "Cut," Allen said. He stood with his hands on his hips, a look of displeasure on his face. "Fellows," he said deliberately, "it wasn't fast enough. This is a space ship. It is not a Spad. You remember the Spad. It's an old World War I airplane. A Spad is not supposed to go faster than a space ship. But it just did." He beamed. "You've got to push, fellows. You've got to put your hearts into it."

The cockpit was rolled back and the greenery replaced. The old fog was blown away and new fog laid down. The bell rang and the stage went silent. Allen called for action and the platform moved slowly forward, the crew straining, the ship gathering speed. "Push," Allen shouted. "Push, put your heart into it, think of the beer tonight, push, push." The platform ground to a halt. "Beautiful," Allen said. "Print it. One space ship crash."

As Allen walked back onto Stage 18, his secretary handed him another glass of orange juice. He sat on a stool in front of his desk and looked at the storyboard of the next shot. The "socialite-swinger," played by actress Deanna Lund, and the pilot of the spacecraft, played by actor Gary Conway, stumble into a laboratory run by a team of giant scientists. Everything in the lab is outsized—pencils eight feet long, books fifteen feet high, file drawers eighteen feet high. The shots of the space travelers would be photographed on the giant set; shots of the scientists would be filmed on an exact duplicate of the set built to normal scale. Use of the two sets demanded the most precise planning. Allen had dozens of Polaroid snapshots of each set so that he could match every camera setup exactly. If both giants and space travelers were to appear onscreen at the same time, the individual shots of each were processed into one strip of film by the optical and special effects department, using a variety of matte, process and split-screen techniques. In the scene scheduled next, Conway and Deanna Lund

were supposed to hide behind an outsized insect box
when they heard the footfalls of the giant scientists approaching the lab. The insect box shot would be filmed
as a separate insert; then, in the Studio's special effects
department, this shot would be reduced and laid over
the insect box as it appeared in the setup of the nor-
mally scaled lab.

Allen yawned and faked a punch into the midriff of
Land of the Giants' associate producer, Jerry Briskin,
who had two actors in tow. Briskin winced and straight-
ened up. "Irwin, what do you think of these two?" he
said.

"Beautiful, Jerry," Allen said. "Who are they?"

"We need two guys for later, Irwin," Briskin said.
"One for the guy smoking the pipe, one to play the scien-
tist."

"Fine, Jerry, fine," Allen said. "If you like them, I'm
not going to examine their teeth, I trust your judg-
ment." He took one of the actors by the arm and pointed
to the storyboard. "Stick around," he said, "I'll show you
how to make movies."

Allen climbed on a camera crane and was hoisted up
near the rafters. He lined up the shot, using a bullhorn
to instruct Conway and Deanna Lund on how to skulk
across the giant desk and shinny up the pigeonholes to
the top, where they were to hide behind a spool of
thread. The thread was to be their means of escape.
They were to knot it around an oversized needle, stick
the needle into the desktop, and let themselves down
hand over hand to safety.

"Let's run through it once from the top," Allen
shouted down.

Conway and Deanna Lund started across the desk top. It was so large that it took up nearly a third of the sound stage. "Good, good," Allen said. "Now up on the drawers. Good. Start knotting the thread. Deanna— now! You hear the giant. Hide, hide, hide. Beautiful, beautiful. Behind the jar now." Allen was peering through the camera. "I'm picking up your fanny, Gary. Move in farther. Deanna, I've got your fanny now. It's lovely, but not for home consumption. Beautiful, we get all this in the master, we're a bunch of geniuses."

The boom was lowered and Allen walked back over to his desk. He was sweating profusely. Conway, an athletic-looking young man with flaring nostrils and a lot of hair, stood hesitantly behind him.

"Irwin, I was wondering," Conway said. "Will that needle hold my weight when I come down?"

"Good point," Allen said. He yelled for the head grip and explained the problem to him.

"No problem," the grip said. "You let Gary wind the thread around the needle. Then you cut away to something else. We'll anchor the thread underneath the needle. We've got a support under there."

"Beautiful," Allen said. He turned to Conway. "Worry no more."

Conway still seemed perplexed. "What about the timing?"

"Don't worry about the timing here," Allen said patiently. "I just shoot for film here. The timing I make later in the cutting room."

"But are we going to be able to match after you cut away?" Conway persisted. "I mean *how*."

Allen took him by the arm and whispered conspiratorially into his ear. "I know a very smart Chinaman, that's how," he said. "Don't worry about it. We'll cut in and out. I'll use an enormous process shot of you in the background and the giant in the foreground."

Conway was not yet convinced. "Don't worry, baby," Allen said. "I could cut to a Chinaman and you wouldn't be aware of it."

Despite its similarity in structure and technique to other cinema verité pix at N.Y. Film Fest's "Social Cinema in America" sidebar event, Frederick Wiseman's The Titicut Follies *differs from them commercially: its four-letter words and prolonged views of male genitalia completely eliminate television as a potential market.*

Daily Variety

Paul Monash stepped out of his bungalow at the Desilu lot in Culver City and let the sun bake into his face. It was only a few yards over to the sound stage where a segment of his new television series, *Judd*, was being shot. The director, Boris Sagal, was setting up a scene, and Monash stood off to the side of the set as the lights and cables and camera were placed. Finally he moved over and began talking to Sagal. The set was a courtroom and there were dozens of extras hovering about. One of the extras, an elderly woman, kept her eyes fixed on the back of Monash's gold, short-sleeved turtleneck sweater. Suddenly she came up and put her arms around his waist. Monash turned around, surprised. For a moment he said nothing.

"Hello, Mother," he said at last.

"I thought it was you," his mother said.

"Keeping you busy?" Monash asked. He was slightly
ill at ease.

"Oh, yes. How's Caren?"

"Fine."

"And the children?"

"Great." Monash paused. "I've been meaning to call
you. Caren's sister is coming next week with her kids."

"That's nice."

"Yes," Monash said.

"Where are you going to put them?"

"Oh, the kids can double up and Caren's sister can
sleep in the den," Monash said.

"That's nice."

Monash examined his watch. "I guess I've got to go."
He leaned over and kissed his mother on the cheek.
"Bye."

"Paul?"

"Yes."

"You're working too hard."

Monash smiled. "Good-by."

Irwin Allen hovered high above Stage 18 on a camera
crane. Down below, an art director for *Voyage to the
Bottom of the Sea* waved frantically to attract his attention. He was carrying a sketch of what looked like a
blob, but which actually was a costume for a marine
monster scheduled to appear in one of the *Voyage* episodes.

Allen finally caught sight of the art director. "It better
be important," he shouted down from the crane.

"I just want you to okay this sketch, Irwin," the art
director said. Allen beckoned for him to send it up.

When it got there, he perused it quickly, took off his glasses, wiped them on his shirt, then looked at the sketch again. "Okay one monster," he said finally. He gave the sketch one more check. "One thing. His mouth. Does a monster's mouth move when he talks?"

The sketch artist looked bewildered. He wiped his arm across his forehead. "We hadn't planned on it, Irwin."

"A monster looks phony if his mouth doesn't move when he's talking," Allen said. "Fix it. A mouth on the blob."

The first week in September, while last-minute trimming was taking place on *Dr. Dolittle* prior to its Minneapolis sneak preview, the publicity department was deep in plans for the picture's West Coast premiere in Los Angeles four days before Christmas. The premiere was scheduled for the Paramount Theater on Hollywood Boulevard and was for the benefit of the Motion Picture Relief Fund. Tickets were $125 per person, part of which was tax deductible. After the premiere, there was to be a black-tie dinner dance in a tent set up in the parking lot behind the Paramount. Initial planning called for 140 tables, seating ten people each, with the catering done by Chasen's. In return for having their names on the menu, manufacturers had donated free cigars, cigarettes, liquor and favors. As a special publicity gimmick, it had been decided to have several of *Dr. Dolittle's* animal stars arrive at the Paramount in chauffeured limousines. All would be in animal versions of evening clothes and would be accompanied by their trainers. The job of acquiring the limousines fell to Perry Lieber, the semi-retired former head of West Coast publicity who was in charge of premiere planning. One afternoon, Lieber called up a large limousine hire agency in Los Angeles and explained the situation.

"It's really cute as hell," Lieber said. He has a boisterous, enthusiastic voice. "The animals are the stars of the picture and they'll be the hit of the evening. Sophie the Seal will arrive in a limo, and she'll be wearing a rhinestone harness and walk right into the Paramount just like she was a star. And Chee-Chee the Chimp, we'll have him dressed up in white-tie and tails and special patent-leather pumps." Lieber listened for a moment. "Oh, yeah," he said. "All the animals will be wearing pants. They better be, or you'll have some messed-up limos."

11

❝ *That's what we come to Minneapolis for,* **❞**

Stan Hough said

There was never any doubt that the Studio would hold its first preview of *Dr. Dolittle* in Minneapolis. Fox considered the Minnesota capital its lucky city; Robert Wise's production of *The Sound of Music* was first sneaked there, and with the enormous success of that picture, the Studio superstitiously kept bringing its major roadshow attractions to Minneapolis for their first unveiling before a paid theater audience. With so much money at stake—the budget of *Dr. Dolittle* was close to $18 million—the Studio was unwilling to hold a sneak anywhere around Los Angeles, reasoning that it could get a truer audience reaction in the hinterlands, far from the film-wise and preview-hardened viewers

who haunt screenings in and around Hollywood. The
plan originally had been to go to Minneapolis on Friday,
September 8, and to Tulsa the following evening, but
early that week the Tulsa screening was canceled. "If
the picture plays, we don't have to go to Tulsa," Richard
Fleischer said. "If it doesn't play, why go to Tulsa the
next night and get kicked in the ass again? You make
some changes, then you go to Tulsa."

Because of the magnitude of *Dr. Dolittle*, the Minneapolis screening attracted twenty-eight Studio personnel from New York and Los Angeles. The major contingent from Los Angeles was booked on Western Airlines
Flight 502, leaving at 8:30 A.M. on September 8. Arthur Jacobs, accompanied by Natalie Trundy, arrived
at International Airport nearly an hour before flight
time. He was tieless and wearing a dark blazer and he
lingered around the escalator coming up from the
check-in counters on the ground floor, greeting members of the Fox party as they arrived. His salutation
never varied. "I'm not nervous," Jacobs said. "I'm not
going to Minneapolis. I'm just here to wave you all good-
by."

"Oh, Arthur," Natalie Trundy said. "Calm down."

"Calm down," Jacobs said. "*Calm down.* You treat me
like one of the dogs." He turned to Fleischer. "We've got
poodles. She treats me like a poodle."

"You're a very nice-looking poodle, Arthur," Fleischer
said.

They milled around the gate, waiting for Flight 502
to be called, Jacobs, Natalie Trundy, Fleischer, Mort
Abrahams, Herbert Ross, the choreographer on *Dr. Dolittle*, and Warren Cowan, who was once a partner of
Jacobs in a public relations firm and whose company,

Rogers, Cowan & Brenner, was handling the publicity and promotion for *Dolittle*. At last the flight was called. As Jacobs and Natalie Trundy walked up the ramp, Jacobs turned to Fleischer and said, "I just don't want to go to Minneapolis. Let's go to Vegas instead."

"It would be less of a gamble," Fleischer said.

Jacobs and Natalie Trundy took two seats at the rear of the first-class compartment. Cowan, a short, pudgy man with constantly moving eyes and a voice that sounds somewhat like Daffy Duck's, sat by himself in front of them and spread the New York and Los Angeles papers on his lap. Jacobs could not keep still. "We land at noon," he shouted up the aisle. "At twelve-thirty, we visit the public library. At one o'clock, the museum."

No one laughed except Fleischer, who tried to humor Jacobs. "At one-thirty, the textile factory," Fleischer said.

"And then we have a rest period between eight and eleven this evening," Jacobs said. This was the time scheduled for the screening.

"What I like about you, Arthur, is your calm," Fleischer said.

"Why should I be nervous?" Jacobs said. "It's only eighteen million dollars."

The trip to Minneapolis was uneventful. Most of the Fox people slept, except for Jacobs, who kept prowling the aisle looking for someone to talk to. It had just been announced in the trade press that week that Rex Harrison had bowed out of the musical production of *Goodbye, Mr. Chips* that Gower Champion was scheduled to direct and Jacobs to produce for release by M-G-M. "It was all set," Jacobs said sadly. "Gower and I even went to Paris to see Rex. We drive out to his house in the country and he meets us at the door. 'Marvelous day,' he says. You know the way he talks." Jacobs put on his Rex Harrison voice. " 'Marvelous day. Bloody Mary, anyone, Bloody Mary.' He gets us the Bloody Marys and then he says, 'Now let me tell you why I'm not going to do *Mr. Chips.*' That's the first we heard about it. It was all set. Well, Gower looks at me, picks up his attaché case and says, 'Sorry, I'm going to the airport, I'm going home.' " Jacobs gazed out the window at the clouds. "It was all set," he said. "*All set.*"

The Fox party was met at the airport in Minneapolis by Perry Lieber, of the publicity department, who had flown in from Los Angeles the day before to supervise the preview arrangements. Lieber approached the task as if it were—and indeed he seemed to equate it with— the annual pilgrimage of the English royal family from Buckingham Palace to Balmoral. There were none of the ordinary traveler's mundane worries about luggage, accommodations and transportation. Lieber had checked the entire twenty-eight-man Studio contingent into the Radisson Hotel, ordered a fleet of limousines to transport each planeload of Fox people to the hotel, and arranged that all baggage be picked up at the airport and sent immediately to the proper rooms and suites. He gathered baggage tags and dispensed them to waiting functionaries and gave each new arrival an envelope containing his room key and a card listing that person's flight arrangements to New York or Los Angeles the next day, as well as the time that a limousine would pick him up at the hotel for the trip out to the airport.

Jacobs took his envelope and gave it to Natalie Trundy. For a moment, he peered intently at Lieber's tie pin, a musical staff on which the words "The Sound of Music" were written in sharps and flats. "You've got the wrong picture," he said.

"Are you kidding?" Lieber replied boisterously. "This is my lucky tie pin. You know how *Sound of Music* did and we previewed that here."

Warren Cowan shook his head slowly. "This has got to be the most superstitious movie company in the world," he said.

"If they're so superstitious," Fleischer said, "then why didn't they get Bob Wise to direct this picture?"

Outside the airport, standing beside a limousine, Natalie Trundy pulled out a Kodak Instamatic and began snapping pictures of the Fox party. She was dressed all in white and was wearing pale yellow sunglasses. She aimed her camera at Cowan, but her flashbulb misfired and she asked for one more shot.

"Oh, for God's sake, Natalie," Jacobs said. "Let's get going."

Cowan sat on the jump seat and opened a copy of the *Minneapolis Tribune* to the theater section, where the Studio had placed a teaser advertisement that did not give the name of the picture. The advertisement was headlined "Hollywood Red Carpet Preview."

"They're charging $2.60 a ticket," Cowan said. "That's a mistake. You want to get the kids at a preview of a picture like this, and at $2.60 a head, it's too steep."

"They should have made it two bucks a couple," Jacobs agreed miserably. At this point, he seemed to see disaster in everything. "To get the Friday night dates."

"It's a mistake," Cowan repeated softly.

As the limousine sped toward downtown Minneapolis, the chauffeur began to issue statistics about the city. "There are fifty-eight lakes and parks within the city limits," he said. No one paid any attention. Jacobs put out one brown cigarettello and lit another.

"Are you going to stand or sit in the theater tonight?" he asked Fleischer.

The director stared out the window at the early autumn foliage. "I'm going to lie down," he said. He patted Jacobs on the knee. "It's only a preview, Arthur," he said.

"Of an $18 million picture," Jacobs said.

Lunch was served in the Flame Room of the Radisson. It was after three o'clock and the dining room was deserted, but the kitchen had been kept open for the Fox group. Many had not yet arrived and others were up in their rooms napping. Jacobs had changed into a dark suit and he bounded from table to table.

"Don't forget, we're due at the art museum at three-thirty," he said.

"Arthur's making jokes," Lionel Newman said. The head of the Studio's music department, Newman had arranged the score and conducted it on the sound track. He had arrived in Minneapolis the day before with a Studio sound engineer to help set up the theater for the preview. "Arthur, as a comic, you're a lardass."

Jacobs looked chagrined.

"You know what I call this hotel?" Newman said.

"Menopause Manor." He smiled at the waitress. "That's okay, honey, I don't mean you. But you got to admit, there's one or two old people staying here. I mean, this hotel talks about the swinging sixties, they don't mean the year, they mean the Geritol set."

Suddenly Jacobs raised his arm and shouted, "The Brinkmans." Standing in the doorway of the Flame Room, with his wife Yvonne, was Leslie Bricusse, the tall, bespectacled young English writer who had written the screenplay, music and lyrics for *Dr. Dolittle*. Jacobs was beside himself. "The Brinkmans are here," he cried to Fleischer. "Brinkmans" was his nickname for the Bricusses. "Did you see them?"

"He could hardly miss, Arthur," Newman said. "You make it seem like the start of World War III."

"Sit over here, Leslie," Jacobs said. He snapped his fingers for the waitress, who was standing right behind him. "We need chairs. Leslie, you want a sandwich, coffee, a drink?"

The Bricusses were pummeled by the Fox people and diffidently gave their order to the waitress. Yvonne Bricusse, a handsome, dark-haired English actress, slipped into a banquette alongside Natalie Trundy, who kissed her on the cheek. She poured herself a cup of coffee.

"What are you wearing to the opening?" Natalie Trundy said.

"New York?" Yvonne Bricusse said.

"Mmmmm," Natalie Trundy said.

"A heavenly thing," Yvonne Bricusse said. "Leslie bought it for me. Autumn colors, sort of. Burnt orange, with a bow here." She patted her bosom.

"Divine," Natalie Trundy said. "How about Los Angeles?"

"Nothing yet," Yvonne Bricusse said, sipping her coffee. "I thought I'd get something made. What do you think of Don Feld?" Feld is a motion picture costume designer.

"Heavenly," Natalie Trundy said. She reached over with her fork and speared a piece of steak off Jacobs' plate. "A lot of feathers, though."

Yvonne Bricusse brooded for a moment. "Mmmm," she said. "I know what you mean. He *does* like feathers." She stirred a spoon lazily in her coffee cup. "What about you?"

"In the works," Natalie Trundy said. "They're on the drawing boards, New York, London, Los Angeles, all the openings." She fluttered her arms like a ballerina. "I'm going to *float*. I haven't even talked about colors yet. I want to see how they look on the board."

That evening, before the preview, Richard Zanuck hosted a party for the Fox group at the Minneapolis Press Club on the second floor of the Radisson. Zanuck had just that day returned from Europe, a combination business and pleasure trip to London and Paris, then a week vacationing in the South of France with David and Helen Gurley Brown. He looked tanned and healthy. "I'm still on Paris time," he said, dipping a cocktail frankfurter into some mustard. "Stopped off in New York this morning to see a rough cut of *The Incident,* then back onto a plane out here."

"You can sleep tomorrow," Arthur Jacobs said.

Zanuck shook his head. "I'm going back to Los Angeles at six-thirty in the morning."

"Why?" Jacobs said.

"I want to go to the Rams game tomorrow night," Zanuck said.

Jacobs looked incredulous. He filtered through the room, stopping at each little group. "Dick's leaving for L.A. tomorrow at six-thirty. In the morning. You know why? He wants to go to the Rams game."

At 7:45, Perry Lieber beat on the side of a glass with a fork. He told the assembled group that the preview started at eight sharp and that after the picture there would be a supper served in Richard Zanuck's suite on the twelfth floor. The picture was playing just down the street from the hotel at the Mann Theater, one of a chain owned by a Minnesota theater magnate named Ted Mann. Fox had rented the theater for the night, paying off Universal Pictures, one of whose roadshow films, *Thoroughly Modern Millie*, was playing there. Three rows of seats had been roped off for the Fox contingent, along with three other seats in the back of the house for Jacobs, Mort Abrahams and Natalie Trundy. Jacobs had specially requested these seats because he is a pacer and wanted to be free to walk around the theater without disturbing anyone. As Jacobs walked into the lobby of the theater, his eye caught a large display for *Camelot*, the Warner Brothers-Seven Arts musical that was to be the Christmas presentation at another Mann house. He stopped in his tracks.

"Oh, my God," he said. He looked at the people spilling into the theater. "Oh, my God, *Camelot*. That's what they'll think they're going to see. Oh, my God."

The house lights went down at 8:13. The audience was composed mainly of young marrieds and the middleaged. There were almost no children present. Zanuck sat in an aisle seat, with Barbara McLean, the head of the Studio's cutting department, beside him, a pad on her lap, ready to take notes. The overture was played and then a title card flashed on the screen that said, "Equatorial Africa, 1845." The card dissolved into a prologue and Rex Harrison, in frock coat and top hat, rode onto the screen on top of a giraffe. There was no murmur of recognition from the audience. Some of the Studio party began to shift uneasily in their seats. The prologue lasted only a few moments. Harrison, as Dr. Dolittle, the man who could talk to the animals, slipped off the back of the giraffe to treat a crocodile ailing with a toothache. He tied a piece of string to the aching tooth and then tied the other end of the string to the tail of an elephant. At a signal from Dr. Dolittle, the elephant pulled on the cord and the tooth snapped out of the crocodile's mouth. Harrison patted the crocodile on the snout, put its huge molar in his waistcoat pocket, climbed on the back of a passing rhinoceros, and rode through the jungle out of camera range. There was not a whisper out of the audience as the prologue dissolved into the cartoon credits. At the appearance of the title *Dr. Dolittle*, there was a smatter of applause from the Studio contingent, but the clapping was not taken up by those who had paid $2.60 a ticket.

Throughout the first half of the film, the audience was equally unresponsive. Even at the end of the musical numbers, there was only a ripple of approval. At the intermission, David Brown hurried out into the lobby. "I want to hear the comments," he said. The noise in the lobby was muted. Most of the people just sipped soft drinks and talked quietly among themselves. Several of the Fox people blatantly eavesdropped on their conversations. Jacobs stood by one of the doors, his eyes darting wildly. Natalie Trundy leaned against him, her eyes brimming with tears, kneading a Kleenex between her fingers. In the center of the lobby, a circle of Studio executives surrounded Richard Zanuck.

"This is a real dead-ass audience," Zanuck said. "But you've got to remember, this isn't *Sound of Music* or *My Fair Lady*. The audience hasn't been conditioned to the songs for five years like they are with a hit musical."

"This is an original score," Stan Hough said.

Zanuck nodded his head vigorously. "And an original screenplay," he said. The muscles in his jaw popped in and out feverishly. "My God, these people didn't know what they were going to see when they came into the theater. The first thing they see is a guy riding a giraffe."

"It's not like *Sound of Music*," Hough said.

"Or *My Fair Lady*," Zanuck said. "Those songs were famous before they even began shooting the picture."

The second half of the picture did not play much better than the first. There was only sporadic laughter and desultory applause for the production numbers. When the house lights finally came on, the only prolonged clapping came from the three rows where the Studio people were sitting. In the lobby, ushers passed out preview cards. Tables had been set up and pencils provided for the members of the audience to fill in their reactions. These cards were more detailed than most preview questionnaires. "PLEASE RATE THE PICTURE," the cards read. "Excellent. Good. Fair." In another section, the questionnaire asked:

> How would you rate the performance of the following?
> *Rex Harrison*
> *Samantha Eggar*
> *Anthony Newley*
> *Richard Attenborough*
> Which scenes did you like the most?
> Which scenes, if any, did you dislike?
> WE DON'T WANT TO KNOW YOUR NAME, BUT WE WOULD LIKE TO KNOW THE FOLLOWING FACTS ABOUT YOU:
> A) Male—Female
> B) Check Age Group You Are in—Between 12 and 17
> Between 18 and 30
> Between 31 and 45
> Over 45
> THANK YOU VERY MUCH FOR YOUR COURTESY AND COOPERATION.

Jacobs wandered through the lobby. His eyes were bloodshot. Natalie Trundy trailed after him. She had stopped crying, but her eyes were red-rimmed.

"I hear the cards are seventy-five per cent excellent," Jacobs said to no one in particular. He watched a woman chewing on a small yellow pencil as she perused her card. The woman wrote something down, erased it, then wrote something else. Jacobs tried to look over her shoulder, but when she saw him, the woman shielded her comments with her hand.

Ted Ashley, the president of Ashley-Famous Artists, Rex Harrison's agents, came up and clapped Jacobs on the back. "Arthur, you've got yourself a picture here,"

Ashley said. Jacobs waited for him to say something else, but Ashley just slapped him on the back again and went over to talk to Zanuck.

"The audience was kind of quiet," Zanuck said.

Ted Mann, the theater owner, a large blocky man at one of whose theaters *Dr. Dolittle* was going to play when it opened in Minneapolis, elbowed his way to Zanuck's side. "I want you to know, Dick, a year's run," he said. "A year minimum."

"I thought the audience was a little quiet," Zanuck repeated.

"Yes, it was, Dick," Mann said. "But it's the kids who are going to make this picture, and we didn't have many kids here tonight." Mann seemed to search for the proper words. "You've got to realize," he said, "that what we had here tonight was your typically sophisticated Friday night Minneapolis audience."

Zanuck seemed not to hear. "They weren't conditioned to it like *Sound of Music*," he said.

"That's my point, my point exactly," Mann said. "But they'll be hearing this score for the next four months until the picture opens. By the time December rolls around, they'll know what they're going to see, don't you worry about that, don't you worry at all."

Jacobs looked over at Zanuck. "Over fifty per cent excellent," he said.

The theater emptied and the Fox party slowly walked back to the Radisson half a block away. There was little enthusiasm as they rode up the elevator to the party in Zanuck's Villa Suite. The suite was enormous, on two levels, with a large living room and two bedrooms on

the balcony above it. A bar had been set up on the balcony and a buffet beside it. The food had not yet arrived. There were only two large bowls of popcorn which
were quickly emptied. The room was quiet, with only a
slight hum of conversation. Jacobs, Abrahams, Bricusse, Natalie Trundy and Barbara McLean sat around
a coffee table totting up the cards, stacking them into
piles of "Excellent," "Good" and "Fair." There were 175
cards in all—101 "Excellent," 47 "Good" and 27 "Fair."
One viewer had written "Miserable" and another noted
that Rex Harrison played Dr. Dolittle "like a male Mary
Poppins." Two women objected to a scene with white
mice and five to another scene in which Anthony Newley drinks whiskey out of a bottle.

"Those broads are all over forty-five, right?" Jacobs
said.

"The 'Fairs' are all over forty-five," Abrahams said.

Ted Mann peered down at the cards. "You've got to
realize that this was a typically sophisticated Friday
night Minneapolis audience," he repeated.

"What we needed was a lot of kids," Natalie Trundy
said. She dabbed at her eyes with a handkerchief and
asked someone to bring her a Scotch on the rocks.

It was obvious that the Studio was distressed by the
results of the preview. It was not just that the cards
were bad—though with $18 million riding on the film,
they were considerably less favorable than the Studio
might have liked. But what disturbed them even more
was the muted reaction of the audience during the
screening of the picture.

"I think it's damn silly to come all the way to Minneapolis and then not tell people what they're going to

see," Zanuck said. "It's all right to have a sneak in Los Angeles. But you come this goddamn far to get away from that inside audience. So tell them what they're going to see. Get the kids out."

Richard Fleischer nursed a drink, stirring it slowly with his finger. "That's right, Dick," he said. "Tell them in the ads." He moved his hand as if he were reading from an advertisement. " '*Dr. Dolittle*—the story of a man who loved animals.' "

"Right," Zanuck said. "They know what they're seeing, they'll break the goddamn doors down." He gave his glass to Linda Harrison and asked her to get him another drink. "When we run it next, in San Francisco, maybe, we'll tell them what they're going to see. No goddamn teaser ads."

"I'd be mystified," Fleischer said, "if I came into the theater and didn't know what the picture was and the first scene was a guy riding a giraffe."

Jonas Rosenfield, the Studio's vice president in charge of publicity, who had come from New York for the screening, edged up beside Zanuck. "It's all true," he said. "But we've all got to admit that this was an invaluable preview. We know now how to promote this picture to make it the big success we still know it's going to be."

"This is what previews are for," Owen McLean said.

"Right," Stan Hough said. "This is what we come to Minneapolis for, to find out things like this."

Waiters arrived and laid out a supper of filet mignon on hamburger rolls. Calls were placed to Harrison in France, where he was making another Studio picture, *A Flea in Her Ear,* and to Darryl Zanuck in New York.

When the call to Darryl Zanuck came through, Richard
Zanuck and David Brown went into a bedroom and
closed the door. The party seemed to settle in. Jacobs
still went through the cards, one by one.

"No kids," he said. "Everyone is over thirty."

"It's the kids who'll make this picture a hit," Harry
Sokolov said.

In a corner of the room, Owen McLean sat down on a
couch beside David Raphel, the Studio's vice president
in charge of foreign sales. "Well, David," McLean said,
"What did you think?"

Raphel, a distinguished-looking middleaged man
with a slight foreign accent, wiped a piece of hamburger bun from his lips. "A very useful preview," he
said carefully. "This picture will take very special handling to make it the success we all know it's going to be.
We mustn't forget the older people. They're the repeaters. The children won't get there unless their grandparents take them. The grandparents, they're the repeaters.
Look at *The Sound of Music*."

"There are people who've seen *Sound of Music* a hundred times," McLean said.

"My point," Raphel said. "My point exactly."

Slowly the party began to break up. It was after one
A.M. and a number of the Studio people were leaving
for Los Angeles at 6:30 the next morning. At the door
of Zanuck's suite, Ted Ashley shook hands with Jacobs.

"You've got yourself a picture, Arthur," Ashley said.
"It's all up there on the screen."

"It'll work," Jacobs said. "Cut a few things, switch a
few things."

"It's going to be great, Arthur," Rosenfield said. He

patted Jacobs on the arm. "None of us has any doubts about that."

Zanuck's suite cleared by one-thirty in the morning. At four A.M. he called Harry Sokolov and told him to round up Hough, McLean and David Brown for a meeting in his room. They convened in Zanuck's suite at 4:45 A.M., and for the next hour Zanuck went over the picture reel by reel. Before the meeting broke up, shortly before six, it was tentatively agreed to cut the prologue. A decision was deferred on whether to cut any of the musical numbers. Arthur Jacobs was not present at this meeting.

12

" *And I think Lincoln is a hell of a part,* **"**

Pandro S. Berman said

The Monday after the Minneapolis preview of *Dr. Dolittle,* the following item appeared in Army Archerd's gossip column in the Hollywood trade paper, *Daily Variety:* "Arthur Jacobs back from Minneapolis getting congrats on the sneak of *Dr. Dolittle.*"

A few weeks later, another item about the Minneapolis sneak appeared in "Walter Scott's Personality Parade" in the Sunday supplement *Parade.* ("Want the facts? Want to spike rumors? Want to learn the truth about prominent personalities? Write Walter Scott.")

Q. My wife caught the sneak preview of the movie *Dr. Dolittle* in Minneapolis, and she says it is slow. Did this picture really cost 20th Century Fox $27 million?

D.T.L., St. Paul, Minn.

A. The film cost approximately $17 million, but with sales and promotion costs added, the company needs $27 million to break even. The *Dr. Dolittle* sneaked in Minneapolis, admittedly too long, has now been edited into a shorter, faster moving version.

The Studio, after the Minneapolis preview of *Dr. Dolittle*, would have liked to cut the picture's prologue in its entirety. It was too long, it did not get the anticipated laughs, it delayed the first musical number until too deep in the film, it did not firmly establish the identity and character of the picture, and it made the long cartoon credits that followed anti-climactic. But eliminating the prologue meant cutting the only sequence in the picture in which Rex Harrison rode the giraffe, and the giraffe with Harrison aboard was the major motif in the Studio's advertising and promotion campaign for *Dr. Dolittle*. With the world premiere in London less than three months away, it would have been prohibitively expensive for the Studio to institute an entirely new campaign. In addition, millions of dollars worth of merchandising gimmicks tied to the giraffe would have had to be scrapped. The problem was how to cut the prologue and keep the giraffe, and it was Richard Zanuck who finally came up with a solution. Late in the picture, after the intermission, there was a sequence in which Dr. Dolittle goes off through the Sea Star Island jungle in search of a giant whale. In the script as written (and the picture as filmed), the scene dissolved with Dr. Dolittle heading off into the jungle, picking him up in the next sequence on the coast of Sea Star Island. Zanuck suggested that the giraffe sequence from the prologue be cut in between these two scenes so that Dr. Dolittle is actually seen traveling through the jungle. The dialogue from the prologue was excised and in Paris, where he was making *A Flea in Her Ear*, Harrison looped new words to cover the giraffe's change in destination. With this detail taken care of, the Studio then cut the rest of the prologue out of the picture. The only remaining problem was that Harrison, in the prologue, wore a different costume than he wore during the island sequences; he disappeared into the jungle in shirtsleeves and one pair of pants, rode the giraffe wearing a frock coat and another pair of pants, and arrived at the coast in the first costume. There was nothing the Studio could do about this. Richard Fleischer, for one, did not seem particularly disturbed by the bad costume match. "Who's going to notice it?" he said. "If they start picking on that, we're dead anyway."

Besides cutting *Dr. Dolittle* for the San Francisco sneak, which was scheduled for late October, Fleischer was also preparing *The Boston Strangler*. At his instigation, the Studio had finally assigned the title role in the *Strangler* to Tony Curtis. It was a piece of offbeat casting. Curtis' career was in trouble. He had gone through a number of agents and appeared in a string of frivolous formula comedies that had flopped at the box office. The good picture offers were not coming in and he was seriously considering a bid to host a television series about detectives, in which he would also appear in a given number of episodes. Curtis was desperate to change his career image from the mindless comedy parts he had done for so many years. When he heard that Fox had bought *The Boston Strangler,* he put in a request to play the part. Mindful of his recent performances, the Studio's reaction was frigid. A number of name actors were anxious to get the role and scores of unknowns had been auditioned. But Curtis persisted. On his own, he had himself made up to look like his conception of the Strangler, fleshing out his nose and features with putty, rearranging his haircut, dressing himself completely in black. In this reincarnation, he had photographs of himself taken and sent over to Fox. The Studio was still cool. But Curtis as the Strangler intrigued Fleischer. In a Studio projection room, Fleischer went over three of Curtis' earlier pictures— *The Sweet Smell of Success, The Defiant Ones* and *The Outsider*—frame by frame. In each, Curtis had played a man driven and on the run. Fleischer was convinced that Curtis was the man to play the Strangler and, together with producer Robert Fryer, he broke down the Studio's resistance. The Studio drove a hard bargain with Curtis. "We have the right but not the obligation to use his name in the credits," Owen McLean said. "It's a gimmick, sure. But in a lot of situations, his name doesn't do anything for you. People might think the picture is just another Tony Curtis comedy."

One afternoon early in October, Fleischer supervised the setting up of a Panavision camera in a corner of Stage 8 for makeup tests of Curtis as the Strangler. The sound stage was empty save for a clutter of struck sets, props and sketched building exteriors. Nervously puffing on a large brown cigar, Curtis picked his way through the props and entered a portable dressing room set up by the stage door. He was wearing makeup and was dressed all in black—shoes, chino pants, turtleneck sweater. He had flown to Los Angeles that morning from Las Vegas, where he was making his first night club appearance, hosting a show starring Tammy Grimes, and he was due back in Las Vegas for the first show that evening. He checked his hair and his makeup and came out of the dressing room arm in arm with Fleischer.

The purpose of the test was to see how Curtis' makeup job looked on film. The bridge of his nose had been built up and his face was slightly puffier. Curtis sat on a stool before a black screen. Fleischer looked through the camera and then went over and brushed some hair from Curtis' forehead. "Can we have the nose shaped a little more?" Fleischer said. "The same profile, but a little thinner."

He went back behind the camera. The film started to roll. An eye-light lit Curtis' face from the nose upward. Slowly Curtis revolved on the stool, stopping, looking, his eyes flashing.

"Now look up, Tony," Fleischer said. "Now down, you hear something, listen, you're scared, but they don't have anything on you. That's right, that's good, once more around, slowly, slowly, okay." He went up to Curtis, who offered him a cigar. Fleischer smiled and shook his head. "That was good," he said. "If we can just shape the nose a little. It looks too much like a prizefighter's now. Too thick. And we should change the hair a little. Make it longer. You know, the Italians are always combing their hair. Make it longer and we can have a lot of business with a comb."

Fleischer asked for another take. This time Curtis circled counter clockwise on the stool. Fleischer shook his head. "Your left side doesn't look so good," he said. "Let's favor the right side today."

After lunch, Curtis left the Studio to return to Las Vegas. In the afternoon, Fleischer returned to Stage 8 to make some camera tests. He had been impressed by the multi-image technique used by the films shown at the Montreal World's Fair, and with the Studio's approval, was going to use the same techniques with *The Boston Strangler*. Instead of using a single frame that covered the entire screen, Fleischer would in certain sequences project multiple panels onto the screen, showing related elements of the same scene played simultaneously. He was planning to get some cut footage to see how the process actually looked on screen before *The Strangler* began shooting in Boston in January. Using two young actresses from the New Talent School, Fleischer shot a number of related scenes from the script—a girl talking on the telephone to a caller making obscene suggestions, her roommate racing to another apartment to get help, a closeup of the caller himself, a boy from the New Talent School. On Fleischer's chair was a storyboard showing how the three individual shots would be juxtaposed on a single frame, with the different panels growing and diminishing in size as the action progressed.

Fleischer gave the two girls as much attention as he would veteran actresses. When he was finished he quietly thanked each. "That was nice," he said.

"Nice, but I still don't know what the hell the scene was all about," the assistant director said.

Fleischer smiled. "It was dirty," he said.

Outside the stage, Fleischer stood in the hot afternoon sun and ran his fingers through his graying hair. "We've never made use of the big screen," he said. "All we've done is take what we used to put on the small screen and make it bigger. And then pictures, all pictures, have always had the same frame. It's like you told every artist in the world that all paintings had to fit in the same sized frame. But with these multiple panels, if you have a horizontal picture, then you use a horizontal frame, a vertical a vertical, an oblong an oblong, all different sizes and shapes."

He leaned down to tie a shoelace and started to walk to his office. "This won't work with every picture," he said. "But it will work with this one. We've got an abstracted story and an abstracted character in Albert De-Salvo." He paused and raised his face to the sun. "Of course, there are all sorts of problems with a new technique like this. You've got to have precise counts or the action on one panel will overlap onto the action of another. You've got to lead the audience without letting them know they're being led. You do it by color, by movement, by action, by size changes in the panels, making them follow the story you want them to follow."

He was engrossed in the process and as he walked seemed to be talking almost to himself. "It's so complicated we've got to use a storyboard for the picture. I hate them. I've never used one before. They're for beginners. But with a technique like this that no one has ever used before, it's the only way you can show your crew what you're doing. And I'm using a cutter who's never cut a picture on her own before. She's been an assistant, that's all, so she doesn't have any preconceived ideas. She's not like a lot of those old cutters, you can't do this, you can't do that, this is how we did it on such-and-such a film. This is as new to her as it is to me and she's been able to come up with a lot of good ideas."

He paused on the steps of his office. "And there's not an abundance of them around," he said.

Though Tony Curtis' wardrobe in *The Boston Strangler* consisted almost entirely of work clothes, he insisted that everything be custom tailored. The assignment fell to costume designer William Travilla, a high fashion *couturier* under his professional name, Travilla, and the designer of Errol Flynn's costumes in some of his swashbuckling and codpiece epics. "I'm not knocking Tony, but he is a pain in the neck to work with," Travilla said one day. "He's such a perfectionist. But I guess it's a very serious picture and the clothes couldn't be handled by just buying a green zipper jacket. We wanted to get as slender a look as possible, so the pants were dropped to the hipbone and made with fewer pockets. Then the work shirts were made to measure so there wouldn't be a lot of bulk to push down into the pants. Then everything was put in the washing machine and mangled so that they'd have character. Oddly enough, the changes we made in the clothes aren't noticeable. The character comes out moody and nasty and certainly doesn't look custom made. The clothes create a more sensuous approach, and after all, the Strangler had to have sex appeal to get into all those women's apartments."

With a start date set for *Hello, Dolly!* the Studio was now turning its attention to other roadshow possibilities. One was a dramatization of Stephen Vincent Benét's poem, *John Brown's Body*. The project had been assigned to producer Pandro S. Berman, who had hired playwright Paul Osborne to do the screenplay. A few days after the first draft of the screenplay was completed, Berman and Osborne were summoned to Richard Zanuck's office to get his reaction.

"Well, Richard, I'm very excited," Berman said. "I think we have an Academy Award winning picture here."

Zanuck cleared his throat. "I'm excited, too, Pandro," he said. He nodded toward Osborne. "I wish all first drafts were this good." There was a speck of cigarette ash on his desk and he carefully swept it into a wastebasket. "There's just one thing. I think we depend too much on narration, you know, on the words of the poem. I wonder if this could be dangerous. I thought I spotted a number of places where action could tell the story instead of narration."

Berman shifted easily in his chair. "As a matter of fact, Richard, I've been cutting the script, cutting what my wife calls the Mickey Mouse action, and the things I've been cutting are just what you've been talking about, the narration."

"It shouldn't be used as a crutch," Zanuck said.

"That's right, Richard," Berman said. "Where the narrator speaks for Lincoln, we can use Lincoln to speak for himself."

"Use scenes instead of narration," Zanuck said.

"My feeling, exactly, Richard," Berman said. "And I'm sure it's Paul's."

Osborne's face showed no expression.

"Let the characters tell the story instead of the god-damn narration, great and beautiful as it is," Zanuck said.

"Keep the poetry but go deeper with the people," Berman said. "So the first order of business in the second draft is to translate the narration into scenes." He turned to Osborne. "Did you get that, Paul?"

Osborne nodded.

"Now I thought the love story is a little shallow," Zanuck said.

"You want some complications," Berman said.

"That's right," Zanuck said. "I want to get deeper into the story. Maybe it can do with a little spice."

Berman smiled thoughtfully. "If I may suggest it, Paul," he said to Osborne, "I think we can give Richard what he's looking for, the sexy angle, by having Clay sleep with Sally." He turned to Zanuck. "Isn't that right, Richard?"

"Right," Zanuck said.

"Now it may be too early," Berman said, "but I've got some ideas for casting."

"It's never too early," Zanuck said.

"Well, I'd like to draw on my old relation with Sidney Poitier to play Spade," Berman said.

"Isn't he a little genteel?" Osborne said.

"Not really, Paul," Berman said. "I had him playing a Mau Mau in *Something of Value*."

"Ah," Osborne said.

"And I think Lincoln is a hell of a part," Berman said.

"I agree, Pandro, I agree," Zanuck said. He fingered the script and cleared his throat again. "There's one small point about Lincoln, though. Do you think it might be too obvious to have someone say to him, 'Are you going to the theater tonight?' "

"I see your point, Richard," Berman said smoothly. "And I think we can cut that. Can't we, Paul?"

At his party for Renee Valente, his new director of talent, Screen Gems President Jackie Cooper explained that company's upcoming special, A Christmas Carol. *"Christopher Isherwood is writing it," he said. "Dickens was a terrible writer. In the original, Scrooge is mean and stingy, but you never know why. We're giving him a mother and father, an unhappy childhood, a whole background which will motivate him."*

Abby Mann denies the rumor that playwright-buddy Arthur Miller is unhappy with Mann's screenplay of After the Fall. *"For one thing," says Abby, "Arthur hasn't even seen it yet. For another, we hope to do another movie together. For a third, Arthur hasn't any contractual control over the movie at all."*

Two items in Joyce Haber's column in
The Los Angeles Times

Late in October, *Star!* was in the final stages of shooting. All the non-musical portions of the picture had been completed and the company had shut down to rehearse the musical production numbers that remained to be shot. Daniel Massey, the young English actor who played Noel Coward in the film, had finished all his scenes but lingered in Los Angeles to loop some dialogue. The day before he was scheduled to return to London, Massey spent the whole morning and afternoon in the looping room in the basement of the Studio Theater. "Looping" means dubbing, and is necessitated by extraneous background noises picked up during filming, the desire to get a different inflection in the actor's voice, or simply because a long shot precluded the use of a microphone. It is a tedious process and is so called because the loop of film showing the scene to be dubbed is run round and round through the projector and flashed on the screen in the front of the room. The actor must watch his image and synchronize his words precisely to the movement of his lips on the screen.

The dubbing room was furnished in what looked like Salvation Army rejects—old chairs and a moth-eaten settee. A microphone was set up and marks put on the floor showing Massey the limits he could move forward or back to adjust his vocal volume. Massey dropped into a chair, puffing nervously on a cigarette. For the first time, he was having some doubts about his portrayal of Coward. "I'm going to be pilloried," he said. "There's no doubt about it. People are going to say I'm just imitating Noel. I'm not, you know. He talks all up here"—he waved his hands up by his temple and talked as if he had a head cold—"not down here." He patted his stomach. "I could imitate him, of course. But that's going the Frank Gorshin route. That's all right for night clubs, but I'm not a mimic."

A voice from the control booth announced that the new loop was ready. The scene was after the opening of Gertrude Lawrence's first Broadway show and Massey, as Coward, was reading the reviews. It had been shot on location at the Algonquin Hotel in New York, but background noises had made necessary a new reading of his line: " 'Jack Buchanan, a young Englishman of astonishing grace and charm.' " Massey slipped to the microphone and listened to the original sound track to get the proper inflection of his voice. He signaled that he was ready and the loop was played without the sound.

" 'Jack Buchanan, a young Englishman of astonishing grace and charm,' " Massey said. He bit each word out.

"You were late with 'a young Englishman,' " the sound man said.

Massey repeated the line.

"A little rubbery," the sound man said.

Again and again, Massey repeated the words. He rolled his "r's" and cut off the word "charm" so sharply it sounded like "charmp."

Finally the sound man was satisfied. Massey listened to the playback. "Okay, I'll buy it," he said. He flopped back into his chair. "Pilloried," he said. He lit another cigarette from the butt of the first. "What's the next loop?"

" 'What price Clapham now?' " the sound man said.

"My God, there must be an easier way," Massey said.

A few days later, after two weeks of rehearsal, director Robert Wise was ready to shoot the "Jenny" number in *Star!* "Jenny" was a Kurt Weill-Ira Gershwin song sung by Gertrude Lawrence in Moss Hart's *Lady in the Dark,* a Broadway hit in the early 1940's. Though it would last only three or four minutes on screen, the number would take two weeks to shoot. A musical pro-

duction number is enormously complicated to film. All
movements must be keyed to a musical count. How,
where and at what pace dancers and principals walk,
jog or leap is determined by the beat. Careful measure-
ments must be made of the distances to be covered in a
particular shot in order for action and camera movement to synchronize with the music. The stage directions in the script gave only a slight indication of the
difficulties involved:

167 NEWSREEL
The newsreel shows the stage on the opening night of
Lady in the Dark. Full of actors dressed as circus performers. The backdrop is a large painted circus scene
which might be used for the cover of a magazine. Upstage the "jury" (consisting of clowns, acrobats, etc.) is
taking their places. Downstage, Gertie, wearing a chic
and glamorous evening dress, moves to take her place on
a trapeze. She is surrounded by the other principals of
the show, including the ringmaster and his page. Gertie
starts to swing gently on the trapeze. We hear the music
of "Jenny," and Gertie, still swinging leisurely on the
trapeze, starts to sing.

GERTIE (*singing*)
"There once was a girl named Jenny
Whose virtues were varied and many . . ."
As Gertie completes this verse, she swings toward
CAMERA and suddenly leaps forward off the trapeze and
right into CAMERA and . . .

168 INTERIOR NEW YORK THEATER NUMBER 4—NIGHT
. . . as she lands on the stage, the screen bursts,
blazes and explodes into widescreen color as Gertie
bursts, blazes and explodes into her brilliant, electrifying
bumps-and-grinds version of "Jenny."

GERTIE (*singing*)
"Jenny made her mind up when she was three
  She herself was going to trim the Christmas tree . . ."

All the musical numbers for *Star!* were choreographed by Michael Kidd, the Broadway dancer and director who was working on his first film in over ten years. A slim, dark-haired man with a nervous athletic grace, Kidd sucked on a cigarette as he moved the chorus back and forth on the stage. Off to the side, Robert Wise sat quietly in a director's chair watching Kidd position the dancers. Kidd bounced back and forth between the facsimile stage and the camera crane where he checked angles with *Star!*'s cinematographer, Ernest Laszlo. The master shot—a shot showing the entire number, taking in all the performers onstage—had already been filmed, and now Kidd was lining up individual movements and closeups. The male dancers were wearing circus costume and dead-white facial makeup offset with ruby rouge spots; the women wore spangled tights. Onstage, Kidd's assistant, a dancer named Sheila Hackett, was standing in for Julie Andrews, practicing a leap from a platform into a male dancer's arms. She did the leap several times as Kidd peered through the huge 70mm camera to make sure that it caught the entire movement.

Wise climbed up on the crane and took a look through the camera. "It's a bit vacant in the background," he said to Kidd. "We're going to pick up a big hole there. You'd better put some more dancers back there, Mike."

Kidd called for some additional dancers, and when

he was finally satisfied, he ordered a break for the chorus to touch up their makeup. Julie Andrews was still in her dressing room. Finally Wise told Reggie Callow, his assistant director, to have the chorus take their places. As one of the male dancers in clown costume passed him, Wise touched his arm. "You're wearing a watch," he said gently. "Clowns don't wear watches. It shows up on film."

"I forgot," the dancer said.

"I'll hold it," Wise said. He took the watch and put it in his pocket.

Julie Andrews emerged from her dressing room as Callow bellowed over a bullhorn for the dancers to take their positions.

"You better sit over here, dear," Wise said to Julie Andrews. "We'll run it through once more so you can see what we're doing."

The camera dollied in for a rehearsal. Onstage, Sheila Hackett waited for the musical playback to begin and on cue leaped from the platform into the dancer's arms.

"We need some more acrobats," Kidd said. "We've still got a hole back there."

"You told me you didn't need any more," Callow said. His beefy red face was rimmed with sweat.

"We only need their legs," Kidd said. "We're only going to pick them up from the waist down. They don't have to wear their tops. Only the bottoms."

There was a momentary delay until the dancer-acrobats took their places. Once more, Sheila Hackett did a runthrough.

"I've got it now," Julie Andrews said. She peeled off her bathrobe and took her position on the stage, wearing a form-fitting black sequined outfit. With Kidd chanting the beat over a bullhorn, she did a practice leap from the platform. The dancer did not catch her just right and she repeated the jump a half dozen more times until the timing was perfected. At last Wise called for a picture. The set went silent and then the pre-recorded music for the number blasted through the stage. Mouthing the words of "Jenny," Julie Andrews leaped from the platform.

Again the dancer did not catch her right, and the shot was repeated. This time Julie Andrews' leap was too high. On the third take she muffed the lyric and on the fourth the dancer once more did not catch her properly. Wise called for another take and then still another. Beads of sweat began to ring Julie Andrews' forehead. After each take a makeup man powdered her face.

The morning wore on. Nearly an hour and a half passed before Wise got the shot he thought he wanted. Then the camera operator said a few words to him.

"Your foot was out of the frame, dear," Robert Wise said then. "Let's do it again."

The company broke for lunch at twelve-thirty. They were supposed to return in an hour, but Julie Andrews had a costume fitting and did not reappear on the set until nearly three o'clock. His elaborate paunch spreading out like a table from under his shirt, Reggie Callow sat in Wise's chair, surrounded by members of the crew.

"You remember Steve Cochran?" Callow said. "Just died a while back. Well, he was the best I ever saw at promoting stuff. A lot of actors, you know, they like to smoke in a scene. But Cochran, he had a piece of business he liked to use, it was the best I ever saw. He liked to *open* a pack of cigarettes. That way, every take you had to give him a fresh pack. I remember one picture, he did nineteen takes of a scene one day, and that night he went home with nineteen packs of cigarettes with just one butt out of each package. That's almost two cartons. Oh, he was something, really something."

"All those stars are something," a makeup man said.

"Something is right," Callow said. "Tight is what you mean. No wonder they're all rich. Nineteen packs of cigarettes." He shook his head. "Sid Mintz told me a story once. He was working over at Paramount, working as Jack Oakie's wardrobe man. Well, when the picture started, Sid tells Oakie he'll take good care of his things. First thing you know, Oakie starts bringing his suits in in the morning for Sid to get cleaned. Not his wardrobe. His suits, from home, from his own closet, so help me God. Then his wife's dresses, then his laundry. Sid tells me he even brings the sheets. Well, when the picture is over, Oakie, he says to Sid, 'You took real good care of me, Sid, go out and buy yourself a good cigar.' And he gives him a twenty-five-cent piece."

The crowd around Callow guffawed. "Oh, I tell you," Callow said, "the true story of Hollywood's never been written. There's so many funny things happen, you wish you had written them down."

He looked at his watch. Julie Andrews' car was sliding down the street. She jumped from the back seat, wearing a long, sleeveless cotton bathrobe.

"Oh, I'm sorry I'm late," she said.

The star had arrived and the desultory swapping of tales about the stars was over for the day.

"Let's go to work," Callow said.

13

You've got to have twelve letters in your name,

Ernest Lehman said

The start of shooting on *Hello, Dolly!* was marked by an exchange of gifts, notes of encouragement and a small champagne and caviar party for Barbra Streisand, who was playing the title role, in the office of director Gene Kelly. Richard Zanuck sent producer Ernest Lehman an additional supply of champagne and caviar along with a note that said:

Dear Ernie,
    You have labored long and hard to bring DOLLY to the starting gate—and I know she will win all the blue ribbons.
    Best of good wishes.

                              Sincerely,
                              Dick

For his part, Lehman sent Kelly a gift of brandy and whiskey, which brought the following note in return:

Dear Ernie,
    Thanks for the opening-day sentiments. We'll give it the old college try and then some.
                    Gene

There was an 89-day shooting schedule on *Hello, Dolly!* and at the end of the first week's shooting, Ernest Lehman still did not have a completed budget. In his five-room suite of offices in the Old Writers Building, Lehman fretted. Worry seems almost endemic to him. He is a slender man in his early fifties with long graying sideburns and thinning hair arranged artfully across the top of his head. He had been a top screenwriter for over fifteen years, several times a nominee for the Academy Award and the recipient of a number of best screenplay awards from the Writers Guild. His last assignment at the Studio was the screenplay of *The Sound of Music*, for which, in addition to his normal salary, he received a token 2 per cent of the picture's profits, a piece that now amounted to nearly a million dollars. *Hello, Dolly!* was only the second picture that Lehman had produced. The first was *Who's Afraid of Virginia Woolf?* and the disparity between the two projects seemed at times to overwhelm him. "I've got some goddamn nerve," he said. "From a four-character picture to this." A pained look crossed his harried face. "You know, there's one sequence where we're going to put out a call for 2,500 extras."

He was wearing a checked jacket and a soft white

Zhivago shirt and on his wrist he wore a thin gold watch on which the letters of his name replaced the numbers, like this:

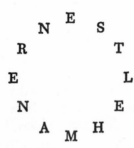

"You've got to have twelve letters in your name," Lehman said. "Otherwise it won't work. And it's best to have six in your first name and six in your last."

He buzzed his secretary and asked her to ring Chico Day, the production manager on *Hello, Dolly!* His wistful eyes rested on the painting of Barbra Streisand that dominated his office. "It's by Claire Trevor," he said, cupping his hand over the phone. There was also a photograph of Barbra Streisand on an end table, in a silver frame that was a gift from Mike Nichols, who had directed *Who's Afraid of Virginia Woolf?* Engraved on the frame were the words, "Hello, Forever. Love, Nichols. *Virginia Woolf.* 1965."

"Chico," Lehman said, when Day came to the phone, "how are we doing on the rain insurance?" *Hello, Dolly!* was supposed to go on location for a month in Garrison, N.Y., and the weather in the East was always a problem. Cover sets were being built in Garrison so that the company could shoot interiors in the event of rain. A prolonged rain spell could be prohibitively costly, forcing a company to shut down and adding as much as several million dollars to the budget of a major picture, only a fraction of which could be recouped by rain insurance.

"We've only got cover for three days, Chico, so I need the figures on what it's going to cost," Lehman said. He listened for a moment, his face growing even more mournful. "You can only get it by the hour? Jesus, if it rains, it gets so muddy you can't shoot all day. An hour's rain is going to cost us a day anyway, so let's try and get this insurance by the day and forget this hour stuff."

He hung up the phone and picked up a stack of publicity photographs of himself, examining each one through a pair of glasses without temples that resembled a lorgnette. "Gee, is my double chin as bad as in these pictures?" Lehman said, patting himself under the chin. "I don't think so." He handed the photographs back to Patricia Newcomb, the public relations woman assigned to *Hello, Dolly!* "See if they can do something with my chin."

The telephone rang. It was Barbra Streisand, soliciting funds for Martin Luther King's Southern Christian Leadership Conference. A number of people in the entertainment business had pledged the SCLC one per cent of their annual income and Lehman was one of those from whom a similar contribution was being asked.

"Gee, Barbra, this is going to be an expensive telephone call," Lehman said. "Why don't you call Freddie Fields? He's rich. Or Dick Shepherd? He's got a lot of that Goetz money."

Late that afternoon, Lehman drove his Cadillac over to Stage 14 where Michael Kidd, who was choreographing *Hello, Dolly!*, was rehearsing the title number with Barbra Streisand. The set was the most complicated interior for *Hello, Dolly!*, and at $375,000, the most costly of all the inside sets. It was called Harmonia Gardens and was suggested by the more lavish restaurants of New York's gaslight era. Lehman's production designer, John DeCuir, had built the set on four levels, foyer, bar, dining room and dance floor. Fittings and furnishings were burnished gold and ivory, and curtains, upholstery and carpeting were crimson, pink and salmon. There were two large 28-foot fountains, twenty columns each ringed with a fountain of its own, four domed private dining alcoves and, dominating the set, a huge staircase. It was at the top of this staircase that Barbra Streisand was now standing, chewing placidly on a hangnail.

She was wearing a lightweight muslin version of the beaded topaz dress designed by Irene Sharaff for the *Hello, Dolly!* number. The purpose of the rehearsal was to see if the dress was functional. Both Lehman and Kidd suspected that the original, still unfinished, was too heavy for Barbra Streisand to execute the high kicks choreographed by Kidd. Standing in the sunken dance floor on the lowest level of the set, Kidd clapped his hands. The male dancers lounging in rehearsal clothes at the foot of the staircase took their positions. Lehman pulled up a stool and perched on it beside Kidd. The music for the number had already been pre-recorded and Kidd motioned for it to begin. Beating rhythm with his hands, he said, "Okay, let's take it from the top."

Barbra Streisand began moving slowly down the red-carpeted staircase, mouthing the words of "Hello, Dolly." "Hello, Rudy. Well, hello, Harry." When she reached the bottom of the stairs, the tempo picked up. The dancers swirled around her, circling the ramp above the sunken dance floor. Twice Barbra Streisand tripped over the train of her dress and twice more the dancers stepped on it. The number concluded, after a complete circuit of the set had been made, with Barbra Streisand, all alone, ascending the staircase. Kidd whistled through his teeth for the music to stop.

"The train's got to go, Ern," Kidd said to Lehman.

"Maybe we'd better get Irene over here," Lehman said hesitantly.

"Sure, Ern, get Irene over here, but the train's still got to go," Kidd said amiably.

A call was put in to Irene Sharaff to come immediately to Stage 14. Lehman fingered the neck of his Zhivago shirt. "Michael, I don't think the number ends right," he said. "I think Barbra should be coming down toward the camera, not going away from it."

"No question, Ern, it stinks," Kidd said pleasantly.

"What I mean, Mike . . ." Lehman began.

"No problem, Ern," Kidd said. "The number's not finished. We're just here to see how the dress works and how the set works."

"It doesn't stink, Mike, that's not what I meant."

"Ern, the number's not finished," Kidd said firmly.

The stage door opened and Irene Sharaff walked onto the set. Winner of five Academy Awards and a number of Broadway awards for costume design, she was an intense, formidable, chain-smoking woman in late middle age. She was wearing a suede miniskirt, foulard blouse and ranch hat, and as Kidd explained the problem with the dress, she sat noncommittally on a stool, puffing on a cigarette.

"Perhaps I'd better see what you're talking about, Michael," she said when Kidd finished. Her tone was deliberate and slightly patronizing.

Kidd motioned for the number to be done again. The music began, and as Barbra Streisand and the dancers circled the set, Irene Sharaff twisted slowly on her stool, following their movements. Again both Barbra Streisand and the dancers tripped on the train of the dress.

"See what I mean?" Kidd said when the music stopped.

Irene Sharaff ground out her cigarette with the toe of her shoe. "No, Michael, I don't see what the problem is."

"It's simple, Irene," Kidd said. "Barbra trips on it, the dancers step on it."

"Perhaps if you changed the movements, Michael, the dancers wouldn't step on it," Irene Sharaff said.

Lehman wiped his brow nervously. Kidd seemed unperturbed. "We've still got Barbra tripping on it."

"I don't think in the finished dress she will," Irene Sharaff said. "The material is so heavy, it flows much better than the muslin."

"There's another problem, Irene," Kidd said patiently. "The dress is so heavy Barbra won't be able to kick at the end of the number."

"But, Michael," Irene Sharaff said as if to a child. "Is the kick necessary?"

"I think it is, yeah," Kidd said. He seemed unfazed by Irene Sharaff's recalcitrance.

"The dress will be finished next week, Michael,"

Irene Sharaff said. "Why don't we wait until we see it on Barbra before we talk about changes?"

"Sure, Irene," Kidd said cheerfully. "And if the dress doesn't work, there'll be some changes made."

Michael Kidd was also unhappy about the set. The dance floor, the lowest of the set's four levels, was in a sunken well bordered with booths and banquettes that were topped with gaslights and curlicue grillwork. The circuit made by the dancers in the *Hello, Dolly!* number was to be on the next higher level, around the rim of the well. But much of the number was going to be shot from the floor of the well and Kidd wanted the booths lining the sunken dance floor ripped out. His reasons were that the diners in the booths and the gaslights and the grillwork would all be in the foreground of the shot, detracting from Barbra Streisand and the dancers doing the number immediately above and behind. With the booths out, the cameras could concentrate on the main action.

"But, Michael, the set is supposed to be a restaurant," said John DeCuir, the production designer on *Hello, Dolly!* and a winner of Academy Awards for both *The King and I* and *Cleopatra.*

"John, I know it's a restaurant, but is the purpose of this set to show a number or to show a lot of people eating?" Kidd said.

"I'm just saying, Michael, that if we take out the booths, then there was no reason making the set a restaurant," DeCuir said.

"And I'm saying, John, that people aren't going to pay $3.50 a ticket to see someone gumming down a lamb chop," Kidd said. He dispatched his assistant, Sheila Hackett, to one of the booths, and then he crouched and squinted in the middle of the well, using his hands as a camera to frame a shot. "See, we've got Sheila right there in the foreground, right? She's a nice kid, but the people aren't paying to see her, they're paying to see Barbra. And Barbra's going to be behind her."

Lehman shook his head in annoyance. "For Christ's sake, why does this have to come up now?" he said angrily. "We had sketches of this set, we had a model of this set, so why didn't you two get together before this? You know what this set cost, you know Stan Hough's on my ass about it, you know we can't spend another goddamn nickel on it, and now you're telling me we've got to rip out some booths."

"I didn't say that, Ernie," DeCuir said.

"Yeah, well, Ern, John likes to look at people eating," Kidd said.

"Oh, for Christ's sake," Lehman said. He walked off by himself for a moment and then came back and asked DeCuir if it were possible to pull out just a few of the booths and not all. DeCuir shook his head.

"I'd have to pull them all out, Ernie, and then put in an apron that comes out about six inches from the present facing," DeCuir said.

"Why that, too, for Christ's sake?" Lehman said.

"We need the apron, Ernie," DeCuir said. "No camera operator is perfect. If his camera jiggles, you're going to pick up the facing, and without the booths, what is there? Nothing. The apron gives us something in front of the dancers' feet, so if the camera does jiggle, we've got some floor space to show."

Lehman slapped his palm on a stool. "Well, can't we have some shots of people in the booths?" he said.

"Sure, Ern, no objection," Kidd said. "We can establish it, we can have a couple of angles shooting up through the booths. Then we take out the booths and shoot the rest of the number."

Lehman looked unhappy. "Find out how much it's going to cost," he said to DeCuir. "And then I'll call Stan Hough. I don't want him on my ass Monday. Let's get him on my ass now and get it over with."

The plans for the various premieres of *Dr. Dolittle* continued to take shape through the early autumn of 1967. Rex Harrison had agreed to leave his home in Portofino, Italy, to attend the openings in Copenhagen, London, Paris, New York and Los Angeles. In line with Harrison's itinerary, Arthur Jacobs wrote a memo to the Studio's New York publicity office:

> Harrison has agreed to make appearances at all airports, theaters, and post-premiere parties accompanied by Chee-Chee and Polynesia. Plans are being made through Mort Abrahams for Ray Kabat to accompany Chee-Chee and Polynesia, plus a second trainer with a stand-in for each animal. They will be booked on the same flights with Harrison so that they can disembark at each city with him.

Like all major premieres in Hollywood, the opening of *Dr. Dolittle* would be covered on television. The usual procedure was to have the show on a local TV channel, and as their limousines pulled up to the theater, the arriving stars would be interviewed by Army Archerd, the gossip columnist for *Daily Variety*. Arthur Jacobs, however, was angling for a national network pickup of the Los Angeles opening and had been in contact with Joey Bishop to host the premiere on his late-night ABC talk show. Bishop's show was broadcast live from a studio in Hollywood for the Eastern time zone and taped for later showing at eleven-thirty the same night for the West Coast. Bishop had expressed preliminary interest in doing the *Dr. Dolittle* premiere, but Richard Zanuck had vetoed the live pickup Bishop wanted.

"What I don't understand is why," Jack Hirschberg said one afternoon in Arthur Jacobs' office. A balding, sad-faced man who always looks on the verge of tears, Hirschberg was the publicity man for Apjac. "You can't buy the kind of exposure you get on Joey's show."

"Because of the *Camelot* opening, that's why," Jacobs said. He was munching on a cracker. "They had Army Archerd out front. Live. And the picture started fifty-five minutes late. You make an audience wait fifty-five minutes and they hate the picture before it even starts. Dick Zanuck says we start at eight o'clock sharp and if we blow Joey Bishop, we blow Joey Bishop. It's disaster to make an audience wait fifty-five minutes. We got to get him to tape it."

Hirschberg's resigned features saddened even more. "He won't do it," he said.

"What time does he go on?" Jacobs said. "Eight-thirty, right? If he goes on live, that means the picture doesn't start until nine-fifteen the earliest. You want to make the audience hate the picture, Jack, you make them sit there until nine-fifteen. They don't get out then until after midnight, they haven't had anything to eat, the hell with the party after, they go home and get a sandwich and they hate us." Jacobs demolished another cracker. "We got to get Joey to tape it."

"He won't do it," Hirschberg insisted.

"What do you mean, he won't do it?" Jacobs said. "We got Rex, Samantha, Newley, Attenborough, Julie Andrews, Burt Lancaster—that's more names than he's had on his show since it started. Of course he'll tape it. That's too big a star lineup to turn down. He tapes it, then we get a helicopter to fly him back to his studio."

Hirschberg shook his head.

"And not just the star lineup," Jacobs said. "What about all the animals arriving in their cars? Of course he'll tape it. Where the hell else is he going to get a chimp arriving in a Cadillac wearing white tie and tails?"

Hirschberg sighed. "Okay, I'll talk to him."

Jacobs rang his secretary and asked for a glass of diet soda. "Now for the party," he said.

Hirschberg checked the notes on his lap. "I've ordered 1,400 albums," he said. "Everybody who comes in gets an album."

"No speeches at the party," Jacobs said. "And the goddamn food at the *Camelot* party was inedible. We've got Chasen's, so that's no problem. But we need two orchestras. The *Camelot* party fell apart because they only had one orchestra. The band took five and everyone left. No wonder, the goddamn party didn't start until twelve-ten." He was back on his original tack. "These are picture people. They got to get up and go to work in the morning. So we can't start later than eight o'clock. We don't want people to get pissed off and leave. Of course Joey will tape it. If he doesn't, Dick Zanuck says it's better to blow the whole show."

The second sneak preview of *Dr. Dolittle* was held at the Orpheum Theater in San Francisco on Friday night, October 20, 1967. In the six weeks since the Minneapolis sneak, the Studio had been at work cutting the picture. The prologue was eliminated entirely, the cartoon-credit sequence pruned drastically and the rest of the film tightened throughout. The night after the San Francisco sneak, *Dr. Dolittle* was to be previewed again in San Jose, and for this showing, two of Anthony Newley's musical numbers, "Where Are the Words?" and "Beautiful Things," had been cut down. The final cut of the picture was to depend on the audience reaction in San Francisco and on the still shorter version shown in San Jose.

After the dead reaction in Minneapolis, the Studio had decided to name *Dr. Dolittle* in the advertisements placed in the San Francisco newspapers for the preview. In both the *San Francisco Chronicle* and the *Examiner*, large three-column ads ran in the theater pages that said:

TOMORROW SOMETHING VERY SPECIAL WILL HAPPEN IN SAN FRANCISCO. Months before the gala world premiere of what will be the biggest reserved seat attraction of 1968, the movie-going public of San Francisco can experience a rare and unforgettable entertainment —tomorrow night at 8:30 P.M., a special advanced preview performance of 20th Century Fox's DR. DO-

LITTLE. You've never seen anything like it in your life
. . . as you enter the wonderful world of DR. DOLIT-
TLE, a world filled with adventure, enchantment, ro-
mance and music. You've never heard such magnifi-
cent music . . . And you'll be captivated by the
performance of Rex Harrison as the incredible DR.
DOLITTLE, the man who can speak some 400 animal
languages from alligator-ese to zebra-ese.

The Fox party was staying at the Fairmont Hotel.
David Brown had come out from New York and Richard Zanuck flew up from Los Angeles in a private jet.
Arthur Jacobs came in from Europe, where he had been
supervising the pre-production details on his musical
version of *Goodbye, Mr. Chips*. Before the preview,
Zanuck hosted a dinner for the Fox party at Ernie's, a
fashionable restaurant not far from the theater. The
executives and production people ate at two large
tables, while the two Studio public relations men attending the preview ate at a small table by themselves.

Natalie Trundy was in an exuberant mood. She
picked up a silver service plate and jiggled it in her
hands, as if to weigh it. "I want one," she said.

"Forget it," Jacobs said. He seemed nervous and ex-
hausted. "I'll call Barney Conrad and he can get us
one."

"Arthur, you miss the point," Natalie Trundy said.

"I don't miss the point," Jacobs said irritably. "Barney
Conrad can get me one. We'll have it by Sunday."

Natalie Trundy pinched Jacobs on the arm and
measured her words slowly. "I want this one, Arthur. I
want to steal it."

Jacobs' eyes circled the table, settling on Mort Abrahams. "Why, for Christ's sake?"

"The thrill is in the chase, Arthur," Abrahams said. He took a silver service plate from an adjoining table and slid it under the tablecloth to Natalie Trundy.

"How do you propose to get it out of here?" Jacobs said. He nodded toward a waiter. "You think that waiter over there doesn't know what you've got on your mind?"

"In my tights, Arthur," Natalie Trundy said.

Jacobs looked perplexed. "I don't have enough troubles," he said. "I got $18 million riding on this picture and you want to walk out of here with a silver plate in your pants."

Natalie Trundy escaped from Ernie's with the silver service plate. The captain pretended not to notice, but added the cost of the plate to the Studio's bill. A fleet of limousines took the Fox party to the Orpheum. A police line had been set up and a crowd of people stood outside the theater gaping at the Studio contingent. In the lobby, Zanuck asked one of the publicity men to get some popcorn and orange drinks for himself and Linda Harrison. Surrounded by Richard Fleischer, Stan Hough and Harry Sokolov, Zanuck looked intently at the audience filing into the theater.

"I told you it was smart to put the name of the picture in the ads," he said. "Look at this crowd. It's a lot younger than Minneapolis."

"You were right, Dick," David Brown said. "We should have done this in Minneapolis."

Abrahams came up to the group. "I've already counted thirty-seven kids," he said.

"I didn't see a single one in Minneapolis, Dick," Brown said. He turned to Sokolov. "From now on, when we have a big sneak, we'll run the name of the picture in the ad, like Dick said."

The Fox party took their seats as the overture began. From the opening credits, it was apparent that the audience was far livelier than the one in Minneapolis. The laughter was not uproarious, but there was a reaction at each comedy sequence and applause at the end of the musical numbers. During the intermission, the Studio party seemed considerably buoyed. David Brown edged through the crowd in the lobby to a covey of Studio personnel.

"I just told Dick cutting the prologue was the logical cut," he said.

After the intermission, the pace of the picture seemed to drag, but the audience still appeared in good spirits. There was a long round of applause when the picture finally ended and the overture was reprised. The preview cards for the San Francisco sneak had been changed and shortened. Unlike the ones used in Minneapolis, there was no space for grading the performances of the actors nor was there space for commenting on individual scenes. As the audience filled out the cards in the lobby, Sokolov pushed his way up to Jacobs, who was puffing nervously on a thin dark cigarette.

"Great, Arthur, just great," Sokolov said. "I've got to admit, I lied to you in Minneapolis. I thought we were in trouble. But this time . . ." Sokolov winked and made a circle with his thumb and forefinger.

The cards were stuffed in boxes and carried back to Zanuck's suite at the Fairmont. A bar had been set up, but there was not enough Scotch and Zanuck ordered up a few more bottles from room service. Jacobs circled the room, trying to get some ice from the empty glasses that littered the suite. Natalie Trundy sprawled on the floor next to Abrahams, stacking the cards. Jacobs picked one up.

" 'Impossibly bad,' " he read. "I would have to pick up that one."

There were some 800 cards in all and Zanuck did some quick figuring. "That's fantastic," he said. "The theater only holds twelve, thirteen hundred people. You figure the people who'll send their cards in by mail, that means practically everyone there made out a card. I've never seen so many cards at a preview."

"It's fantastic, Dick," Brown said.

"Fantastic," Hough said.

The cards broke down to 457 "Excellent," 218 "Good" and 125 "Fair." Sitting at a coffee table, Abrahams pulled out a pencil and a piece of paper and calculated the percentages, comparing them to Minneapolis. He began to frown and calculated the percentages once more, checking them again against the Minneapolis figures.

"How's it work out?" Jacobs said.

"I can't figure it out," Abrahams said. "We're only a percentage point off. Fifty-six per cent 'Excellent' in Minneapolis, 57 per cent 'Excellent' here."

Jacobs looked deflated. "I thought with all these cards we'd be better."

"You know it was a better audience," Zanuck said. "We all know that."

"I could feel it," Brown said. He began riffling through the cards, picking out the "Excellents" and one or two on which the viewers had scrawled comments.

"Here's one, Dick," he said. " 'Good for the whole family.' That's what we like to see. That's money in the bank, Dick."

In a corner of the room, Fleischer was going through the cards by himself. "Most of the 'Goods' say the picture was too long," he said. "With the cuts we have for San Jose tomorrow night, all the 'Goods' will be 'Excellents.'"

Jacobs poured himself another drink. "I don't know about 'Where Are the Words?'" he said. "I hate to lose it. It's a good number."

"Arthur," Zanuck said, "you've got to stop thinking about numbers. You've got to think about the whole picture. A shorter picture is a better picture."

Dr. Dolittle was previewed for the last time the next night in San Jose. Along with the cuts made for the San Francisco preview, the musical number "Where Are the Words?" was eliminated entirely and another Anthony Newley song, "Beautiful Things," trimmed to the bone. The cards at the small theater in San Jose were the best of all three previews, and after viewing them, Zanuck decided to freeze the picture. It was the San Jose print that was to be shown at the world premiere of *Dr. Dolittle* in London on December 14.

14

" *I hear this picture is something,*

a really wonderful picture, **"**

Joey Bishop said

The day before Darryl Zanuck left for England and the London premiere of *Dr. Dolittle*, the first snow of the year hit New York. Slush clotted West 56th Street outside the main office of the Twentieth Century Fox Film Corporation. The Studio's headquarters are in a cheerless warehouse-like building on the far reaches of the West Side, between Ninth and Tenth Avenues, surrounded by seedy tenements and boardinghouses. The interior of the building is as cold and anonymous as the slum outside. The light is bad, the hallways like a maze, the slow, creaky elevator more suitable to moving sides of beef than people. Darryl Zanuck's office on the third floor seems about the size of a jai-alai court and has roughly as much personality. There was, the day I visited him there, a twelve-clock console on a shelf behind the desk, a covey of Oscars and Thalberg Awards, a Picasso and a Van Gogh (both copies) and, dominating the office, a large dark cigar behind which sat Darryl Zanuck. He was dressed all in gray—shirt, suit, tie; the only hint of color was the rosette of the *Legion d'Honneur* in his buttonhole. A puff of cigar smoke drifted toward the ceiling like a small mushroom-shaped cloud and Zanuck began to talk, nonstop, his monologue pitted with detours, but somehow always to the point, the point being himself, not himself in the abstract, but himself as Czar of the Twentieth Century Fox Film Corporation.

"I'm so goddamn sick of being written about," he said. "What the hell am I going to say about myself that I haven't said before?" He adjusted his sunglasses. "Of course, I was disappointed after Minneapolis. It was a bad preview. But I hadn't lost confidence in the eventual outcome of the picture. Dick sent me a wire. 'I haven't lost confidence,' he said. We know what was the matter with the picture now, and it taught Dick one thing. Never take distribution people or sales people to a preview. I've been telling him that for years. They don't know a goddamn thing except selling pictures and they're not going to do you any good going around with long faces in Minneapolis or any other goddamn place."

Zanuck rolled the cigar around in his mouth and then flicked a mountainous ash into the ashtray. "We've got $50 million tied up in these three musicals, *Dolittle*, *Star!*, and *Hello, Dolly!*, and quite frankly, if we hadn't made such an enormous success with *The Sound of*

Music, I'd be petrified. You're never sure of a hit in that category. You're never sure of a hit any goddamn time, but when you're talking $20 million, it's a bigger gamble. You take a picture like *The Sweet Ride*, I don't bother with anything like that. I concentrate on the roadshows and the potential roadshows, who are we going to cast, what do you think of him, what do you think of her? I'm at work at eight o'clock in the morning. It's afternoon in Europe, for Christ's sake, you've got to be. You never get your telephoning done otherwise. I can call London, the operator's number is 11348, I just dial her and give her the number, I'm connected in three, four minutes. You dial Rome, the goddamn Italians make you wait an hour sometimes. Then I'm on the telex six or seven times a day to Dick, when it's afternoon here, it's morning out there, and if I want to talk to him about something special, I just pick up the phone and call him."

As if to prove his point, Darryl Zanuck picked up his telephone and had his secretary place a call to Richard Zanuck in Los Angeles. The Studio operator said that the younger Zanuck was at lunch, and Darryl Zanuck said, "Well, try him at the commissary, for Christ's sake, he's got a telephone there." A moment later Richard Zanuck was on the line.

"How are you?" Darryl Zanuck said. "It's snowing like hell here." There was a pause. "Listen, I got your wire on Elmo. I'll see him in Tokyo, one day, maybe two, but I don't want him in my hair all the time I'm there. Did we close on *The Klansman*? Let's hold it in abeyance. Did Abe tell you about *The Sand Pebbles*? It's the only picture in the whole goddamn country, that and *Gone With the Wind*. Did you know that David Selznick used dummies in the Gettysburg scene? The Actors Guild sued him."

Zanuck hung up the phone. "I was put under terrific criticism when I sent Dick out to head up the Studio," Darryl Zanuck said. "What could I do? He was the only one I could trust. What was crippling this company was the disloyalty, the fighting between the money people in the East and the picture people in the West. We don't have that anymore. I'm the only studio president who's been a producer, a director, a writer and an editor. Who knows the goddamn business. Well, when I took over, I cleaned house. I knew things were bad, but not that bad. I paid off millions of dollars in contracts and threw out every goddamn script we had in preparation. They were all lousy. And then I sent Dick out there. I let him alone. In the first place, I was so goddamn swamped here. And then I thought if I went out there myself, I'd be cutting the ground out from under his feet. People would say, 'Hell, the old man is here, Dick's just an office boy.' So I let him alone. He calls me, he talks me into some things, and I talk him out of some things, I'm a picture maker, and we've done all right."

There is not so much paternal pride in Darryl Zanuck's voice as there is pride in his own executive acumen. He had picked a man to go to Los Angeles, the man had done the job he was asked to do, and the man incidentally was his own son. Darryl Zanuck tossed away his spent cigar and lit another. With $50 million tied up in musicals, there were other film cycles to consider. "We think Malcolm X is a wonderful story," he said. "He was a wonderful man." A cloud of cigar smoke masked his face. "He preached non-violence and they killed him. He was just the opposite of Carmichael and all those other wild men. A picture like this can make a social contribution. Like *The Snake Pit*. After I made that, eleven states changed their laws about insane asylums. And *How Green Was My Valley*. It was laid in England, but it was the first picture to attack unfair unionism."

In his own office down the corridor from Darryl Zanuck's, Jonas Rosenfield, the Studio's vice president in charge of public relations, watched his secretary hang up her snow-soaked coat. He picked up his phone and dialed the number for the weather report, flicking a button on his intercom so that the forecaster's voice filled the room. "Good afternoon," the woman's voice said. "U.S. Weather Bureau forecast for New York and vicinity, 2 P.M. Central Park reading. Temperature 30 degrees, barometer 30.36 and falling. Snow this afternoon and early evening, ending later tonight with a possibility of two to three inches."

"Not bad," Rosenfield said. "Not bad." He speaks with a soft Texas accent and wears suits that seem too big for him, giving him the appearance of a slightly fallen soufflé. "Send a wire to Denton at the Studio," he said to his secretary. " 'Please advise tomorrow whether editors of *Lui*, French Playboy magazine, acceptable for interviews with Raquel Welch. Regards.' "

On his desk were the latest figures on the gross receipts of *The Sound of Music*. "Ninety-eight million dollars," he said. He repeated the figure again, this time more slowly. "Ninety-eight million dollars." Rosenfield shook his head. "I don't imagine we'll give that too much publicity. The theater owners and distributors are already after us to cut our admission prices for the picture. They know we've made a fortune and we haven't gone into general release yet. It's still a hard ticket. So when they hear about $100 million, they'll be after us even more." A slow smile spread across his features. "No, I don't think we'll give that much publicity."

He opened a folder and took out some publicity photographs of Anthony Quinn and Michael Caine, who were in Europe making a film adapted from John Fowles' novel, *The Magus*.

"It's not a winning title," Rosenfield said. "I went to our ad agency and asked them to research some new titles for me." He tossed me a memo that contained four pages of new titles for *The Magus*, among which were:

The Love Faker	*Faker of Life*
Faker of Fate	*A Game for Gods*
Naked Power	*Villa of Torment*
The Fate Twister	*Villa of the Conjurer*
The Goddess and the Demon	*Valley of Yesterdays*
Seduced by Fate	*The Dream Faker*
The Conjurer	*Trial by Sorcery*

"None of them quite hits the spot," Rosenfield said. "But we'll come up with one."

He dialed the Weather Bureau again to get a new forecast, wondering aloud if the snow would delay Darryl Zanuck's plane to England and the *Dr. Dolittle* premiere.

I asked how the Studio set its distribution schedule and Rosenfield leaned forward, tenting his fingers under his chin. "We put out twenty-four pictures a year, plus two roadshows, so it takes a lot of planning," he said. "Of course, a lot depends on the delivery date of the picture, but we pretty much know how we're going to handle a film even before shooting begins. You figure that the big grossing life of a picture in general release is ninety days. After that, it just slides downhill. And the peak period for your heavy grossing is that ten-week span between mid-June and Labor Day. You try to get your biggest commercial attractions into the theaters during that period. Your second big period is Thanksgiving through Christmas. If you're lucky, you get two big holiday spurts. Roadshows you save for the fall. You start building up momentum with the advance ticket sales, and of course you give a roadshow more promotion, so that by the time it opens it hopefully has already built up a head of steam. The questionable pictures you save for the off months. That doesn't mean they can't hit big, they just take different handling, special handling. Take *The Flim Flam Man*. Drop that in during the summer and you get run over. As it happens, it didn't do well anyway, but a picture like that is a controlled disaster. You don't have that much invested in it going in, and your print costs and promotion costs are hedged against results."

I asked if critics had any effect on the success of a picture. Rosenfield shook his head disparagingly. "The more commercial the picture, the less the power of the critic," he said. "If you open up in an art house, they can kill you if they don't like your picture. But what the hell. You've got so little invested anyway, they can't break your back. A big commercial picture's a different story. A critic doesn't mean a hoot in hell." He rummaged through his desk and found a copy of *The New*

York Times. "Take a look at *Tony Rome,*" he said. "The people who hated it said it was tawdry and dirty. They're what I'd call money reviews." He opened the *Times.* "This is the third piece they've run on *Tony Rome,*" he said. "The third time they've called it dirty. That doesn't hurt the box office one bit. That's only for the good."

Guess who's coming to dinner with the Rex Harrisons on Christmas Day? Their colored maid, Ruby, that's who. I had the pleasure of meeting Ruby when I dined with Rex and Rachel on my last Coast visit, and I know how devoted they are to each other.

Radie Harris, The Hollywood Reporter

After four years of blood, sweat and tears, *Dr. Dolittle* finally opened in London at a Royal Command Performance on December 12, 1967. The reviews in the daily newspapers were generally enthusiastic, although the weekly press was far more restrained. In Los Angeles, the Studio immediately reprinted the best of the London reviews in an advertisement prepared for both trade papers, *The Hollywood Reporter* and *Daily Variety.* In Hollywood, however, the word-of-mouth was still bad, and the Studio was immensely gratified when the following item appeared in Joyce Haber's column in *The Los Angeles Times.*

There are certain cliques in Hollywood which seem to prosper on spreading the rumor that a movie is disastrous before it's even been shown—sometimes even while it's in the shooting stage. The venom springs from envy, of course, the envy of one man for another's potential success. The more "spectacular" the movie (all-star and high budget), the more potent the maker's possible success: nasty rumors have been circulating for months about *Dr. Dolittle*. The reviews of *Dolittle* in London, where it opened last week, have put the lie to our local wags. What WE say remains to be seen—but the British are notoriously tough critics, and they gave Arthur Jacobs' $18 million movie the highest plaudits of any American film in a decade. Only possible exception: *Bonnie and Clyde*.

A week to the day after the London premiere, *Dr. Dolittle* opened in New York. In *The New York Times*, Bosley Crowther said that " . . . the youngsters should enjoy it" and that the intermission was " . . . thoughtfully inserted at just about the right place." There was little else, however, that Crowther found in the picture's favor. "The music is not exceptional," he wrote, "the rendering of the songs lacks variety, and the pace, under Richard Fleischer's direction, is slow and without surprise. Indeed, toward the end it is perfunctory. Things happen mechanically. The actors appear self-conscious and the fantasy is dull." *Time* Magazine said that "size and a big budget are no substitutes for originality or charm," and even the trade paper, *Daily Variety*, which depends on advertising from the studios, said the "pic suffers from a vacillating concept in script, direction and acting. . . . Temptation is strong to call it over-produced."

MEMO:
TO: Arthur Jacobs
FROM: Jack Hirschberg
As a result of meetings today between Perry Lieber and myself, the following has been decided regarding the Academy Award campaign for *Doctor Dolittle*.

1. We will screen at eight o'clock each night for the following branches of the Academy: art directors and costume designers, cinematographers, film editors, music. Each screening will be preceded by champagne or cocktails and a buffet dinner in the Studio commissary. We may also arrange to provide soft drinks at the theater during intermission.

2. There will be a meeting Tuesday afternoon of the department heads in Stan Hough's office which Perry and I will attend. At this meeting, Perry will discuss pertinent matters with the department heads and inform them that *Dr. Dolittle* is the Studio's prime target for Academy Award consideration.

MEMO:

TO: Arthur Jacobs

FROM: Jack Hirschberg

Yesterday I sent you a memo outlining our plans for screenings of *Dolittle* for those branches of the Academy who ballot early: art directors and costume designers, cinematographers, film editors and music.

The following notes develop from a meeting today with Perry Lieber to develop an approach for writers, directors and other branches who ballot at a later date.

1. Nominating ballots for writing, directing, best picture and some other categories will be mailed by the Academy January 26. Polls close February 9, by which date all ballots must have been returned to the Academy. Therefore we are booking the Studio Theater every night —if possible—between January 22 and February 6 inclusive. This may be somewhat of an overkill, so to speak, but we can always cancel some dates if we don't need them.

2. We estimate the following membership in the various branches concerned:

Directors	150
Writers	250
Executives	200

Publicity	200
Short Subjects	125
At Large	175
Administrators	100
Producers	150

This totals, according to my faulty logarithms, 1350. Multiply it by two and we will need 2700 seats. At comfortable capacity of the Studio Theater, this spells seven screenings—but we will have to protect ourselves, hopefully, by having the facility available for other screenings as well.

3. In addition, we plan special screenings for various guilds and unions who give their own awards—notably the Editors, Writers and Directors. These screenings will absorb some of the people who will also be Academy voters, but those Academy members who miss their Guild screenings can come to ours at the Studio. So we are covered at least two ways.

The Studio's Academy Award exploitation plan for *Dr. Dolittle* was highly successful. Despite mediocre reviews and lukewarm box office returns, the picture garnered nine Academy nominations, including one for Best Picture, and in the final balloting won two Oscars, for Best Song ("Talk to the Animals") and Best Special Visual Effects. Arthur Jacobs was only momentarily dispirited by *Dr. Dolittle's* reception. In the spring of 1968, his production of *Planet of the Apes* was released and quickly became one of the biggest non-roadshow successes in the Studio's history. Fortunately for Jacobs, *Planet of the Apes* and *Dr. Dolittle* were not "crossed," or cross-collateralized, a common industry practice in which the profits of one picture are used by the studio to offset the losses of another. So great in fact was the success of *Planet of the Apes* that the Studio and Jacobs announced plans to film a sequel. And in London, late in May, Jacobs and Natalie Trundy were married. Less than two hours after the ceremony, according to a report in one of the trade papers, Jacobs was in a business meeting about his musical version of *Goodbye, Mr. Chips.*

With the completion of *The Sweet Ride*, the Studio was unable to find any new properties for Joe Pasternak to produce and he checked off the lot. The film received bad notices and was saturation-booked into drive-ins and neighborhood theaters across the country. A press release said that Pasternak was "reading scripts" and would soon announce a new studio affiliation. In July, 1968, *Star!* opened at a Command Performance in London and received enthusiastic reviews. But when the picture opened in New York, the reviews were, at best, bad. None of the denunciations, however, affected the Studio as much as the quiet, unemotional review by Renata Adler in *The New York Times,* who coolly dismissed *Star!* in less space than she would ordinarily give to a second-feature beach movie. Shooting ended on *The Boston Strangler* and the Studio, having shelved the Malcolm X story, assigned Richard Fleischer to direct *Che!,* a film biography of the late Ernesto "Che" Guevara. ("No one had ever heard of Che Guevara until he died," Fleischer was quoted as saying in *The New York Times Magazine.*) The Studio closed the New Talent School, keeping only a handful of the young actors and actresses, including Linda Harrison, under contract. The Studio also paid $400,000 for an original screenplay called *The Sundance Kid and Butch Cassidy.*

Paul Newman was signed to play Butch Cassidy and the picture was retitled *Butch Cassidy and the Sundance Kid*. The film was assigned to the slate of Paul Monash, who was also keeping busy as executive producer of the television series *Judd* and *Peyton Place*. At Monash's instigation, a Negro family was written into *Peyton Place*'s continuing cast of characters for the first time. "I'm writing a great deal in this area," he told *Daily Variety*. "It's very important—and important also for the future of this show." A Negro writer named Gene Boland was hired to help with the dramatization of the black characters and was very shortly fired after complaining that white writers were rewriting his work. "Boland did not succeed, in our opinion, as a writer for *Peyton Place*," Monash said.

Late in the spring of 1968, Richard Zanuck announced that over the next year, the Studio would spend $115 million on twenty-three pictures. This figure was up 15 per cent over the amount spent in 1967. Nearly 80 per cent of this total, Zanuck said, would be spent in the U.S., most of it in Hollywood. "One, the best technicians are in Hollywood," he explained. "Two, we are not stopping overseas production, but are cutting down on it because the subject matter of the stories involved can be made here and better. This doesn't mean that if we have a foreign locale we won't go abroad to make a film. It is all based on subject matter."

But all that was later. On December 21, 1967, at the Paramount Theater on Hollywood Boulevard, the Studio showed *Dr. Dolittle* for the first time in Los Angeles at a $125-a-ticket premiere to benefit the Motion Picture and Television Relief Fund. I went to the premiere, and I did not go back to the Studio after that, for the point of the Studio is the Product, and during the months I had spent there, the major Product, the $18 million Product, was *Dr. Dolittle*. Limousines were strung out along Hollywood Boulevard and a police line held back a crowd of hundreds straining to see the 1,400 guests who swept into the theater in jewels and evening dress. Governor and Mrs. Ronald Reagan were there as the guests of Richard Zanuck, and Sophie the Seal disembarked from her limousine wearing a diamond necklace. She was accompanied by Jip the Dog, who was wearing a jeweled collar. Gub-Gub the Pig wore a sequined harness and Chee-Chee the Chimp was in white tie and tails with a top hat and white carnation.

Tony Curtis was there and Gregory Peck and Steve McQueen, and in the lobby of the Paramount, Joey Bishop, who had been prevailed upon to tape the premiere for his late-night talk show, interviewed them all.

"This is a real Hollywood premiere," Bishop said. "It's all furs and jewels and delicate hair styles, and that's just the ushers." There was a roar of laughter. "Here's Hank Fonda, Henry Fonda, ladies and gentlemen, Hank, I hear this is a marvelous picture, a wonderful picture."

"A wonderful picture, Joey," Henry Fonda said.

"Thank you very much, Henry Fonda, ladies and gentlemen," Bishop said. "And here's Carol Channing. Look at those jewels."

Carol Channing laughed and waved at the crowd.

"It's a wonderful picture, you're going to see a wonderful picture," Bishop said.

"It's going to be a wonderful picture, Joey," Carol Channing said.

And Rex Harrison said it was a wonderful picture and Samantha Eggar said it was a wonderful picture and Gregory Peck, who was chairman of the Motion Picture and Television Relief Fund, said he was proud that the Fund was the beneficiary of such a wonderful picture.

"And here comes Sonny and Cher, ladies and gentlemen," Bishop said.

"Wow, look at those outfits. Sonny, Cher, come on over here." Sonny and Cher eased their way to the microphone next to Bishop. Sonny was wearing a pale blue brocade ensemble and Cher a floor-length Russian broadtail dress.

"Those clothes are something, really something," Bishop said. "And I hear this picture is something, a really wonderful picture. Everyone's talking about it, and I know you're going to have a wonderful time."

"It's going to be a wonderful picture, Joey," Sonny said.

"So let's see the picture," Cher said.

ABOUT THE AUTHOR

A native of Hartford, Connecticut, educated at Princeton University, John Gregory Dunne now lives in Los Angeles with his wife, Joan Didion, and their daughter, Quintana.